THE SACRED WILDERNESS OF PASTORAL MINISTRY

Preparing a People for
the Presence of the Lord

DAVID ROHRER

IVP Books

An imprint of InterVarsity Press
Downers Grove, Illinois

InterVarsity Press
P.O. Box 1400, Downers Grove, IL 60515-1426
World Wide Web: www.ivpress.com
E-mail: email@ivpress.com

InterVarsity Press® is the book-publishing division of InterVarsity Christian Fellowship/USA®, a movement of students and faculty active on campus at hundreds of universities, colleges and schools of nursing in the United States of America, and a member movement of the International Fellowship of Evangelical Students. For information about local and regional activities, write Public Relations Dept., InterVarsity Christian Fellowship/USA, 6400 Schroeder Rd., P.O. Box 7895, Madison, WI 53707-7895, or visit the IVCF website at <www.intervarsity.org>.

Scripture quotations, unless otherwise noted, are from the New Revised Standard Version of the Bible, copyright 1989 by the Division of Christian Education of the National Council of the Churches of Christ in the USA. Used by permission. All rights reserved.

While all stories in this book are true, some names and identifying information in this book have been changed to protect the privacy of the individuals involved.

The image on page 18 is used by permission of Monk Michael of St. Athos and Aperges & Co. <www.aperges.com>. The image on page 113 is by Matthias Grünewald, from The Yorck Project/Wikimedia Commons. The image on page 163 is used by permission of Saint Catherine's Monastery, Sinai, Egypt.

Cover design: Cindy Kiple
Interior design: Beth Hagenberg
Images: Lake and mountains: © Michael Shepherd/Trevillion Images
    Mountain Symbols: © Nishan Sothilingam/iStockphoto

ISBN 978-0-8308-3824-0

Printed in the United States of America ∞

Library of Congress Cataloging-in-Publication Data

Rohrer, David, 1957-
   The sacred wilderness of pastoral ministry: preparing a people for
the presence of the Lord / David Rohrer.
       p. cm.
   Includes bibliographical references and index.
   ISBN 978-0-8308-3824-0 (pbk.: alk. paper)
   1. Pastoral theology. I. Title.
   BV4011.3.R64 2012
   253—dc23
                                                                        2011051591

P   18   17   16   15   14   13   12   11   10   9   8   7   6   5   4   3   2   1
Y   27   26   25   24   23   22   21   20   19   18   17   16   15   14   13   12

*To the congregation of Michillinda Presbyterian Church
in gratitude for their invitation to labor and learn among them
and to the ministry interns at University Presbyterian Church
in gratitude for the opportunity they gave me
to reflect on what I learned.*

CONTENTS

ACKNOWLEDGMENTS

We have been told that it takes a village to rear and educate a child. My experience tells me that a similar observation can be made about writing a book. I am deeply grateful for the community that has surrounded me over the years and supplied me with the resources I have needed to write this book.

I am grateful for the teachers whose ideas weave their way into this material. The lectures of Ian Pitt-Watson of Fuller Seminary, James Loder of Princeton Seminary and Father Gregory Elmer of the Benedictine community at St. Andrew's Abbey in Valyermo, California, and the books of Eugene Peterson, James Torrance and Andrew Purves have helped me shape a theology of ministry. I am sure I quote from all six of them quite freely without giving credit. So I acknowledge them here and thank God for the way their words have taken root in me in such a way that they are now a part of me.

I am grateful to the congregations I have served. From the people of Community Presbyterian Church of Ventura, California, Michillinda Presbyterian Church of Pasadena, California, and University Presbyterian Church of Seattle, I received gracious invitations to come and labor among them.

In each of these places, people have trusted me and tolerated me, to the extent that they have created a space for me not only to render service but also to be nurtured and invited to grow into a deeper awareness of God's call in my life. Apart from the work that God did in me through service in each one of these places, I have no standing to write this book.

I am grateful to the folks at InterVarsity Press who gave me the opportunity to write and helped me think through the contents of this book, especially Dan Reid, Cindy Bunch and Drew Blankman.

I am grateful to Jake Medcalf, Kyle Turver and Eric Dirksen, three newer leaders in the church who reviewed this manuscript and made comments that guided me in the process of revision. I also want to thank Sue Dryer for her editorial work and her gifts of thoroughness and patience that enabled her to create an index.

Finally, I am grateful to my family. Their interest in this project and their encouragement to persevere is a big part of bringing it to fruition. I give thanks to God for my wife, Mary Ann, my son, Justin, and my daughter, Laura. Each of them in their own way has supported me, chided me and given me a joyous respite from the work of being a pastor. My family has taught me that apart from being a disciple of Jesus, I have no hope of being an effective pastor. My family has taught, and keeps teaching, me how to answer Jesus' invitation to grow in love.

INTRODUCTION

When I was ordained twenty-nine years ago, my mother commissioned a photographic portrait to mark the occasion. As I look at that portrait today, sometimes it's hard for me to believe that I am the one who occupies the frame. It's the kind of photograph you might see hanging in the narthex of some church. It could be very comfortable among a gallery of portraits that detail a congregation's history of pastoral succession.

A younger version of myself stares out at me from this portrait. I am wearing a black clergy robe trimmed with red piping. The robe is adorned with the red velvet cowl of my academic hood. My eyes make direct contact with the viewer, and my half smile suggests a confident but humble readiness for the work that is before me. I am seated, and my hands gently rest on the table in front of me, loosely gripping the primary tool of my trade, a Bible.

I look at this eight-by-ten glossy, and I see the picture of my hope of becoming a venerable statesman in the church. The work before me seemed clear. I would preach and teach, marry and bury, guide and preside. I would take up a noble profession of providing spiritual leadership to the members of a stable institution. I was ready to embark on a career, and I was confident that the journey would be a steady ascent toward bigger and better congregations.

The young man I see in this portrait seems poised to assume his place in that narthex gallery of ministers. However, after twenty-nine years in pastoral ministry, I must confess that it is very difficult for me to identify with this version of myself. What I realize today is that the image of pastoral ministry represented in this portrait probably hit its zenith sometime near the end of the Eisenhower administration. It represents some expectations about the church that are no longer true. Occupying a venerable role in a stable institution is not at all how I think of my job as a pastor. Rather, I see myself as a crewman on a vessel sailing in stormy, turbulent waters who is grateful for the still points we encounter and the glimpses we catch of our destination on the horizon.

The Church: Seeking Survival

Rocked by the waves of a changing culture, the church in America seems to be dealing most with the question of its institutional survival. As leaders in this church, our primary concerns are shifting to matters of maintaining market share. Rather than being the home of theologians, the church seems more to be a test group for sociologists and statisticians. Massive amounts of our energy are being dedicated to diagnosing our disease and tirelessly working to come up with a cure.

As a part of the declining Protestant mainline, it feels at times to me that we are like the knight in the film *Monty Python and the Holy Grail,* who, having been mortally wounded in a sword fight, ignores his hemorrhage and confidently declares himself to have "just a flesh wound." Yet clearly, the best that we, who occupy places of leadership within the mainline, can say about ourselves is that we are "not dead yet."

Other players have come on the scene, offering potential solutions to the problem of decline. The megachurches with Disneyland-sized parking lots, business-park buildings and a full course of religious and spiritual services waiting to be consumed are the churches that are growing in this country. On the other end of the spectrum are the emergent churches that are flying just under the radar. These stealth churches seek to design and deploy "relevant" worship styles and to work to build "authentic" community. Then there is the cry from our seminaries for us to become missional churches. In a "post-Christendom" culture, we are called to see ourselves not as static institutions but as outposts for the rejuvenation of disciples who are being sent into mission.

The eight-by-ten narthex-glossy pastor has little hope of surviving in this brave new world. He is about as relevant in today's church as a typesetter is to today's printing industry. We cannot do the work of pastoral ministry living under the mistaken assumption that we are simply a class of persons known as "the clergy." We are no longer simply theologians and providers of traditional pastoral services within a relatively stable institution. We are now also called on to come to the aid of this struggling institution and to help reshape it. Those of us who are part of the mainline need to wake up to new cultural realities that will influence the way we "do church," and we can learn about these things from the many church planters who are out there experimenting with new forms.

The Pastor's Role: Beyond Survival

Yet irrespective of our church tradition, or our lack of one, we must not let this discussion about the shape of the church dominate our identity as pastors. As pastors we don't primarily exist to build and maintain the institution of the church. We exist to do a particular work through the church. In short, we don't simply have an institution to create, refine or maintain. We have a gospel to preach.

Amid the heated exchanges about how the church should look—or the enormous amounts of energy we spend talking to and about ourselves—it is all too easy to neglect the work that is at the root of our calling. As pastors, we are about much more than the management of a thing; we are charged with proclaiming and demonstrating the healing reality of God's steadfast love in Christ to broken and thirsty people. Yet rather than uniting around this common calling, we are splintering over the questions about the means by which we accomplish it.

The debate polarizes us into the camps of traditionalists and entrepreneurs. The traditionalist voice calls us to ignore observations about cultural developments and give ourselves to the classic duties of parish work. The entrepreneurial voice calls us to deemphasize those tasks and give ourselves more fully to the work of market research and trying to create an attractive brand. But neither the call to return to "the way things were" nor the invitation to create and sell a new form of church will help us navigate the crisis in today's American church. The decision about what kind of pastor we will be cannot be limited to a choice between Mitford and Madison Avenue.[1]

---

[1] I am referring here to Jan Karon's series of novels about the Mitford parish, set in the

In an age that calls on us to rethink how we are going to be pastors in the church, we cannot shed the basic work that makes us pastors. However, neither can we ignore the cultural context in which we do our work. It may be that we have to do more thinking than we'd like about matters of organizational development and the character of contemporary ecclesiastical institutions. Yet we cannot allow our answers to those questions to define the essence of our work. Perhaps Jesus' advice about rendering to Caesar what is Caesar's and to God what is God's is applicable to this situation as well. We have to accept the world's current reality but never lose sight of the greater reality that will one day overcome it.

John the Baptist: Unaffected Yet Effective

What seems to be getting lost in the rancor of this discussion of how to make the church better is a description of pastoral work, a theology of ministry that gives shape to our work irrespective of the kind of church in which we labor. What we need is a pastoral theology adequate for the task before us. We need a philosophy of ministry that is both unaffected by the contemporary situation and absolutely applicable within it. I don't think we'll find this in the writings of the church fathers and mothers who led us during the Eisenhower administration. Nor will we find it in the sociological analyses that tell us why we are in decline. We need to dig a bit deeper to find this substance. In fact, I propose we go back to one who was in ministry during the first century, who himself was a sort of throwback to folks who were in ministry during

---

American South. The books tell the stories of Mitford's lovable Episcopal rector who seems not unlike a contemporary version of some of Jane Austen's vicars.

the mid-eighth century and early sixth century B.C.

I believe that John the Baptist can give us guidance in these matters. He called for both personal renewal and institutional reform. He spoke into a world that was awash with religion but disconnected from authentic relationship with God. He addressed the emptiness of religious institutions that did little more than anesthetize people through empty ritual. He preached a message about the integration of faith and life. Like the Old Testament prophets who went before him, he called the people of his day to live lives that demonstrated a vital covenant relationship with God. Or as John himself put it, "Bear fruits worthy of repentance" (Lk 3:8).

John was profoundly uninterested in religious practice that was not rooted in overt acts of love, love of God that worked itself out in love of neighbor. The baptism that he proclaimed was the sign that gave witness to an internally transformed life. He had had enough of the superficial anesthetic of ritual cleansings that took place in the temple, and so he called on people to come back out to the wilderness to start over: repent, reestablish a covenant relationship with God, return to the place where that relationship was formed and let God once again guide you across the Jordan and into the Promised Land.

People loved it. So they came out to the wilderness around the Jordan to hear him preach and to receive his baptism. John was wildly popular in his day and respected by people as diverse as Jesus, Herod and Josephus. Why? Because he spoke the truth with integrity. Because his ministry was about something bigger than himself or the reform of a religious institution. Because he affirmed what people already knew: that they were in desperate need of something more than the mundane practices of a religion that had been cut off from its source of life.

In Luke's account of John's birth, the angel Gabriel explains to John's father, Zechariah, that John will be about the work of "mak[ing] ready a people prepared for the Lord" (Lk 1:17). In this phrase I believe we have the kernel, or perhaps stem cell, of the essential character of pastoral work. John is going to call people to wake up to God. He is going to remind people that their lives primarily have to do with God. He is going to call attention to the truth that will one day bend every knee and loose every tongue.

"Make ready a people prepared for the Lord." It's a simple thing. Yet this profound piece of the pastoral task is so simple that it suffers from the fate of getting lost. Perhaps it is so readily affirmed as central to our task that we fail to talk about it and about how to do it in today's church. And this is a tragedy, because this phrase is the kind of thing that can help us organize our work. It is a set of lenses through which we can view and evaluate our work. It gives us a simple tool by which to gauge the effectiveness of our work. It provides us the opportunity to ask, Does this thing that I am doing call people to pay attention to God, or not?

In the subsequent chapters of this book I hope to explore the implications of wearing this set of lenses. By looking mainly at Luke's rendition of John the Baptist's story, we see a case study of pastoral work that teaches principles that are translatable for any age. But these principles are especially relevant to our age. In this day when pastors are daily tempted to buy remedies guaranteed to help save the church or products guaranteed to grow a church, we need to be called back to an awareness of why the church exists.

I have no desire to belittle or discount any of these remedies or products. Many of them may be necessary to the church of our day. But if we are to use them, they need to be deployed in service of a greater mission than saving an institution. They need to be evaluated and modified by this greater mission of calling people to wake up to God.

Humbly, Confidently Pointing the Way

About ten years ago, a missionary from our congregation who was returning from service in Albania brought me the gift of an Eastern Orthodox icon of St. John the Forerunner. When he gave me the gift, he also gave me a short course on icons and their use in prayer. He said, "An icon is supposed to point you to God, invite you to prayer. If you look at John's hands in this icon, you'll see what I mean." With both hands

John is motioning to his right. With his right hand palm up and his left hand palm down, he is gently directing our attention to someone other than himself. His head is deferentially tilted in the same direction. His eyes, however, are cast down; it is as if humility will not allow him to make eye contact with the One to whom he is pointing.

It didn't take long to see that it was an illustration of John's famous line about the ministry of Jesus in the third chapter of the Gospel of John: "He must increase, but I must decrease" (Jn 3:30).

Images of what a successful pastor looks like change with the age. Whether it is the narthex-glossy pastors of the midtwentieth century whose sanctuaries were filled with the fruits of the baby boom or today's megachurch hip pastors with their fauxhawks and black T-shirts who preside over auditoriums packed with the young and the restless, we all have in mind some image of what it means to be successful as a pastor. I want to propose John the Baptist as one such image, not because I believe pastors today should take up an ascetic lifestyle or become outlandish to attract people's attention, but because John understood that he was about something that was bigger than himself and bigger than the institution he was seeking to reform.

It is St. John the Forerunner's subtle gesture in the direction of Jesus that compels me to write this book. The humble gentleness and powerful confidence represented in the tilt of his head and motion of his hands have given concrete shape to my work as a pastor. Believing and acting on the truth that the simple work of giving witness to Jesus is one of those still points that can sustain and stabilize us in the otherwise tumultuous voyage of today's church—that is what drives me to get this down in writing.

Thus my intention in this book is not to write a manual on pastoral ministry. I am more interested in fostering a conversation among pastors: first, an internal conversation in which we each reflect on what God is doing in us through this calling, and second, an external conversation in which we help each other turn down the volume on the incessant and anxious appeals to save the church and instead direct our attention to the Lord of the church.

I also hope to do here for new pastors what Eugene Peterson did for me in my early years of ministry.[2] I dare to prescribe a particular set of lenses through which we can view and evaluate pastoral work. I hope to contribute to the conversation concerning the things that give shape to the way we do pastoral ministry in this age. In these days when we are spending so much money, time and energy in the task of healing or growing the church, my hope is that we will see that our work is less about saving the church and more about proclaiming the presence of God to both the souls who compose it and those who dwell outside it.

---

[2]Eugene Peterson's books on pastoral ministry that were especially helpful to me were *Five Smooth Stones for Pastoral Work* (Atlanta: John Knox Press, 1980), *Working the Angles* (Grand Rapids: Eerdmans, 1987) and *Under the Unpredictable Plant* (Grand Rapids: Eerdmans, 1992).

1

CONSOLATION

Making Ready a People
Versus Being the Parson

He will turn many of the people of Israel to the Lord their God.
With the spirit and power of Elijah he will go before him, to turn the hearts
of parents to their children, and the disobedient to the wisdom of the
righteous, to make ready a people prepared for the Lord.

LUKE 1:16-17

Pastor Goes Postal"—I've never seen this headline on the front page of a newspaper. Yet it would not surprise me if someday I did. Looking back on my years in pastoral ministry, I can recall times when I am glad I did not have an automatic weapon at my disposal. While I don't think I was ever angry enough to fire directly at members of the congregation, the thought of shooting out a few windows in the sanctuary in the presence of the gathered congregation has crossed my mind.

What is it about congregations that can arouse such rage in us pastors?

I am still embarrassed as I recall a time about twenty years ago. I was serving a small congregation of older adults in Pasadena, California. It had more than its share of "little old ladies," even for Pasadena. Many of them were the widows of Presbyterian ministers who lived in one of the denomination's retirement facilities a mile from the church. One morning, about four years into my tenure there, I can remember feeling stuck. Stuck in this little church. Stuck in a place where it seemed few, if any, appreciated and understood me. Stuck preaching sermons to sleeping deaf people. Stuck in a church set on one of the busiest corners in the San Gabriel Valley, but that still somehow remained strangely invisible to the world around it.

Lost in my sense of injustice about these things, I looked out at the members of the congregation as they arrived for worship. Mavis was the first to come into view. Ninety years old and still able to make it to church, she was hobbling in, assisted by her walker. The expected "pastoral" response to seeing her ought to have been a grateful exclamation: "How wonderful that you were able to come!" However, in this moment she became for me an archetype of all that was making my life miserable. And in that moment, just before I rose to do the call to worship, I imagined myself walking up to her, pushing her down and throwing her walker out into the busy traffic speeding up and down Rosemead Boulevard.

Now, Mavis had never done anything to me. She was a sweet lady. Why in the world would I ever imagine such a thing? Obviously it had nothing to do with Mavis. It had to do with me. I was furious. Enraged by a long list of unmet expectations and unfulfilled dreams. Angry because of all that was not right about my ministry. And that was the problem: it was *my* ministry. My work there had less to do with God's work among the congregation than with my own perceptions of who I needed them to be and how they ought to respond to me.

The Narcissist in the Pulpit

It is not fun to wake up to one's own narcissism. Yet if the truth be told, there is no small supply of it among those of us who are members of this guild of pastoral professionals. What is it about pastoral ministry that attracts narcissists? Or perhaps the question is, what is it about the office that produces them?

I can think of answers to both questions.

Narcissists are attracted to the office because it puts us front and center every week. At the appointed hour we ascend the pulpit and have at least the feigned attention of our congregations for twenty or thirty minutes. It is a heady experience to have the eyes and ears of a congregation fixed on you. And from that pulpit perch, it is not hard to begin to believe that people have come to worship primarily to hear us. So we begin to give them more of what we think they want: more of us—our opinions, our advice, our exhortations, our stories, our *wisdom*. Tragically, the broad and open space of the kingdom of God is exchanged for the tiny world of the pastor.

Yet the greater tragedy is that congregations seldom complain. And this is how the office nurtures narcissism in its occupants. Why is this? How could a congregation possibly benefit in such an exchange? In a word, congregations can fall into the trap of thinking they need a *parson*. They need to vicariously live the faith through the lives of God's man or

God's woman in front of them. The benefit of having a parson is that she can model the faith and so inspire the people of a congregation to take up the discipleship journey.

Yet having a parson live the faith before you can also be little more than a spiritual anesthetic. It's much less strenuous for members of a congregation to listen to stories of the pastor's encounters with God than to listen for how God might be speaking directly to them. It's much safer to listen to the pastor's expositions of a text than it is to take the risk of entering the strange world of the Bible and exposing oneself to the power of the Word of God. It's much easier to watch someone walk the way of Christian discipleship than to take the journey oneself.

This is what systems folks refer to as a pathological symbiosis. The two entities, pastor and congregation, sustain their relationship with one another by fueling their respective pathologies. The narcissistic pastor gets his ego massaged under the guise of a selfless and sacrificial "ministry." And the anesthetized congregation dreams about the spiritual life while altogether avoiding encounter with the living God. Everyone settles into a rather mediocre and painless place. In this environment, there is none of the discomfort that results from being challenged. But neither is anyone hearing or answering the invitation into relationship with the God who "is able to accomplish abundantly far more than all we can ask or imagine" (Eph 3:20).

If a congregation is in decline, the negative effects of this symbiosis grow worse. The primary mission project of a declining congregation is often the financial support of the pastor. More than once I have witnessed the dynamic of a congregation whose main work is to minister to its pastor.

The spiritual myopia produced by this dynamic is stifling to a congregation. In such congregations, members are called on to give sacrificially for the sake of the church. Yet the missional vision that lies at the root of the call is so small that little energy is mustered by it. Furthermore, the few who do rally to this call ultimately find themselves in a place of fatigue, frustration and resentment when they eventually notice how few of their fellow congregants are joining them in their mission.

The pastor who lives within this dynamic doesn't fare much better, either becoming a sponge who is all too ready to soak up the good will of the "caring" congregation or an angry reformer ready to lash out at people who aren't doing enough to "turn the church around." The fuel for both outcomes is narcissism. In the case of the former, the burned-out pastor who has been broken by the stress of the work willingly becomes the congregation's project. In the case of the latter, the achiever pastor who needs to build a new congregation begins to see the members of his congregation as little more than the workers who need to be mobilized to make this happen. In either case the pastor becomes the center of attention. The illness or vision of the pastor becomes the mission of the church, and neither pastor nor congregation ever make themselves available to the larger work of God.

At best, the parson is one who models Christian discipleship. At worst, he or she becomes captured by a cult of personality and once in this bondage has no choice but to relinquish the prophetic role. Yet it is in this prophetic role that pastors are most likely to be God's tool in the transformation of people's lives. It is when pastors see their work in terms of "mak[ing] ready a people prepared for the Lord" that they begin to apprehend the prophetic dimensions of the pastoral calling.

The Prophet in the Desert

As I look at the life and ministry of John the Baptist, I do not see a man who had any energy for maintaining a religious symbiosis between pastor and parishioner. The kingdom was far too big for him to attempt to press it into this small mold. If anyone lived by the maxim "It's not about you," it was John the Baptist, who said, "After me comes a man who ranks ahead of me because he was before me." "He must increase, but I must decrease." "I am the voice of one crying out in the wilderness, 'Make straight the way of the Lord'" (Jn 1:30; 3:30; 1:23).

For John, this work of making ready a people prepared for God took the shape of a classic Old Testament prophet. He exposed the emptiness of the way things were. He pointed out the weaknesses and foibles of the cultural assumptions and religious practices of his day. He called people to turn from these ways and toward God. John gave himself to the work of giving witness to the God who had created humanity for relationship with himself, and he invited his hearers to respond to God's ever-present invitation to enter into this covenant relationship. In short, John drew people's attention to the presence of God and trusted that doing so was the most important work he could do.

The New Testament writers clued us in to this when they equated John's ministry with the words of Isaiah 40. It was John's role to come alongside his people with the announcement of the good news that God was about to come alongside them. He answered the call to "comfort" God's people with the disturbing and yet reassuring news that God was coming to dwell with them.

Comfort Through Discomfort

It is in the command to bring comfort (Hebrew: *nakhamu*; Greek: *parakaleite*) to the people that we find the stem cell for pastoral work. The sense of this word, variously translated as "comfort" or "consolation," speaks to the action of coming alongside another for a specific purpose. It is the image of showing up or walking with another to give witness to the truth. It is a word that puts together the actions of proclamation and presence. And in the context of Isaiah 40, and the New Testament quotation of this text, it is a word that is used in conjunction with the task of giving witness to the presence of God.

The comfort the prophet is called to bring people is the news of God's coming. And in this way, it is news that is not necessarily comfortable. This kind of consolation is not merely about giving aid to another through empathy and compassion. It is not necessarily comfort that is associated with gentleness and patience. It is the consolation of knowing that God is making his way to his people, and when God shows up, one can expect the landscape to change (see Is 40:4). The valleys are lifted and the mountains are leveled. In short, God's arrival is never without incident. It has massive implications, and if people hear and respond to this word, they find themselves on a brand new road—a road built on the transforming truth that life is about covenant relationship with God.

Like other prophets before him, John the Baptist showed a willingness to shake things up. He spent a good bit of his energy helping people see the vacancy of what they had come to accept as the norm. He told the truth. Doing so got him in trouble with some people, but it also made him wildly popular. Yet in the face of this popularity, John did not build a new movement with himself at its center. Instead he maintained a tenacious dedication to the mission of directing people's attention to God. Like his prophetic predecessors, he gave himself lavishly to the work of simply calling people to wake up to the power and grace of a covenant-making God.

Cleansing for Renewal and Relationship

John's particular tool or window into this awakening process centered around the practice of ritual washings or temple purification rites.[1] As the Gospel writers tell us, he came preaching a "baptism of repentance for the forgiveness of sins" (Mk 1:4). By inviting people out to the wilderness surrounding the Jordan River, he engaged people in a reflection on their life in God. In effect, he got them to consider the question of whether or not their acts of religious devotion in the temple through various ritual cleansings actually reflected some kind of inner change in their hearts. Like Isaiah's admonition about religious festivals and Hosea's message regarding the rites of sacrifice (Is 1:14; Hos 6:6), John's call was for religious practice to match a corresponding renewal of the heart.

The bottom line of John's preaching can be summarized in

---

[1] For a full discussion of this see Joan Taylor, *The Immerser: John the Baptist Within Second Temple Judaism* (Grand Rapids: Eerdmans, 1997). Taylor's study demonstrates the ways in which John gave himself to the work of reforming temple practice rather than creating a new movement with himself at the center. See especially chapter two, "Immersion and Purity."

two questions: Are you aware of God's presence or not? And if you are aware, what difference is this awareness making in the way you are living your life? It was a sort of "put up or shut up" challenge. Marketers of today would have probably advised against it. But oddly, this message made John extremely popular in his day. I would venture to guess that this was true because authenticity sells—then and now. When people come to the end of their rope or hit a dead end, they begin to be open to receive real help. Often this openness begins when people hear someone name their emptiness or identify their inadequacy. The word of comfort is best heard in the wilderness.

Thus the place John chose to deliver his message was as significant as the message itself. "The wilderness," or "the region around the Jordan" (Lk 3:2, 3) was a place of rededication. It was the place where the accoutrements of religion were stripped away. It was the place of beginnings. The Jordan River was the water through which the Israelites had passed to claim the Promised Land. Through John, it became the frontier over which the people crossed to claim a new life lived in response to the promise and presence of God.

To go out to receive John's baptism in the wilderness surrounding the Jordan was a way of saying, Let's go back to the basics. Let's get to the root of what really matters. Let's talk about our covenant relationship with God and how that has an impact on the choices we make in all of our relationships every day. Let's deal with the truth that all the religious washings in the world can't get at.

People are ready to hear good news when they have faced up to the bad news. For this reason, the voice of God is often easiest to hear in the wildernesses of our lives. We are ready to be encountered by the Other when we've had more than enough of ourselves. John's ministry tapped into this reality and in so doing made people ready for an encounter with God.

Resorting to a Cheap Imitation

In some ways it was nothing more than Old-Time Religion: "The kingdom of God has drawn near, repent and believe the good news." And perhaps this is what makes us reticent to resort to it as pastors today. In our anxiety about keeping the church going, we do what is supposed to sell. We resort to a kind of biblicized "how-to-ism" that is not all that different from what populates many of the shelves at Barnes and Noble or is broadcast regularly on the Oprah Winfrey Network.

There is usually nothing morally wrong with these messages. In fact, abiding by them can often lead us to a higher quality of life. But they aren't about God. They don't direct people's attention to God. They are about us and how we need to work harder at what will bring health or well-being. When as pastors we make it our primary job to share these formulae with a congregation, we are taking a profound step away from the core truth that ought to fuel our work. Worse, we are setting ourselves up to be the delivery system for saving truth. We make the mistake of believing the lie that our advice is what people need in order to attain success.

It is the work of a prophet to come alongside others and invite them to wake up to the truth that God has come alongside them. Prophets call people to repent: to turn around and see the God who created us for relationship with himself and has been pursuing us since the foundation of the world. This is the consolation that makes a difference in people's lives. It is the invitation to rest in the ultimate comfort that only God can provide.

Furthermore, proclaiming this consolation makes a difference in the life of the pastor. The anger that is the fruit of our narcissism is allayed when we understand ourselves to be a part of this bigger work. This is primarily because people's response to us and to our ministry moves out of the forefront of our consciousness. The people to whom we deliver this message of consolation have business to do with God, and whether or not they do it is beyond our control.

The Angry Pastor and the Non-anxious Pastor

Until the sights and sounds of Mavis's mangled walker came crashing into my imagination, I had no awareness of just how angry I was. About a year before, someone had pointed it out, but at that time I couldn't see it. I was attending a seminar along with a hundred other pastors that was being offered by the Alban Institute. The subject of our discussions was how family systems theory could be applied to the congregation. On one day, Speed Leas, who was teaching the seminar, talked about Edwin Friedman's notion of how congregational change comes about slowly through the "non-anxious presence" of the pastor.[2]

In the midst of his explanation, my hand shot up with an impatience that was apparently impossible for him to ignore. When he called on me, I offered something that was more of a statement than a question: "How is it that we can be without anxiety when we are regularly being called on to attend and throw holy water on absurd functions like the annual

---

[2]See Edwin Friedman, *Generation to Generation: Family Process in Church and Synagogue* (New York: Guilford, 1985).

luau of the women's association! What does this stuff have to do with the kingdom of God?" At that point Leas walked up to me, put his hand on my shoulder and, addressing the whole class, asked, "Do you hear the anger?"

I didn't hear the anger. Even after being publicly called out, inside I was saying, "I'm not angry; I'm right. These people I work among have a deep problem, and they don't seem to be the least bit concerned about hearing my solutions for it. So don't give me that crap about non-anxious presence. Just give me some tools for how I can get through to them."

He was giving me some tools. But in order to be that non-anxious presence, I was going to need to remove myself from my chosen place of believing that I was at the center of the solution. What I keep learning in the practice of ministry is that the way I make ready a people prepared for God is simply to invite people to wake up to God. My job is to sound the call to turn around, to come down off the myriad of cultural mood enhancers that cloud our awareness and to take note of this God with whom our lives have everything to do. In teaching, counseling, preaching, praying and presiding, I need to be asking, How is God revealing himself to us, and what difference does that make in how we will live our lives?

A passionate dedication to the singularity of this question can transform our ministry as pastors—and make us non-anxious. When people believe that every moment of their lives has everything to do with the living God, watch out! The face of the landscape does change, because what you have is a congregation comprised of people who are expecting to see—and who are therefore available to be a part of—God's work.

2

CALL

God's Work Versus Our Vision

Zechariah said to the angel, "How will I know that this is so?
For I am an old man, and my wife is getting on in years." The angel replied,
"I am Gabriel. I stand in the presence of God, and I have been sent to speak to
you and to bring you this good news. But now, because you did not believe
my words, which will be fulfilled in their time, you will become mute,
unable to speak, until the day these things occur."

LUKE 1:18-23

There have been times in my twenty-nine years of pastoral ministry when I have felt like the better preparatory professional degree for the work might have been an MBA in marketing rather than a master of divinity. We might commence our work with a declining congregation using terms like *spiritual renewal* and *revival* to describe our objectives, but this very quickly devolves into discussions of financial solubility and market share.

In the first three years of my time with the congregation in Pasadena, worship attendance had almost doubled and we had taken in more new members in those years than in the previous ten years combined. It seemed that we were on our way. Or more specifically, it seemed to me that I was on my way. I was accomplishing what I had set out to accomplish. My vision of "turning the place around" was in the process of being realized. The negative trends were reversing. The number of younger faces looking back at me from the pews was increasing. Several younger families had joined the church. Students from Fuller Seminary were coming to worship and asking to serve as interns. The ship had left the harbor, and we were steaming toward our new destination.

But then the ship hit an iceberg.

It actually wasn't as dramatic as that. It happened slowly. It was more like the ship ran out of fuel and began to glide slowly to a stop. Over about six to ten months, most of our growth trend not only stopped but began to reverse. The younger families who had come in started to leave. As they finished graduate school, received jobs in other cities or realized that they needed to move further east to afford a home, they pulled up stakes and moved on.

What I had failed to recognize when they joined the church was that they were people "on the way," and what I learned was that this congregation would only be a place for them to receive hospitality before their journey took them on to a new place. My hope had been that they would join me in my grand vision of building a new congregation on that busy corner. But what I discovered is that most of them were going to be a part of someone else's vision.

Vision. All the books on leadership tell us that we need to have one. But whose vision? I had a vision for that congregation, and I looked at almost every person and situation through the lens of that vision. The couple next door were potential new members. The young PhD in psychology was a leader who could help us assess our organizational and system dynamics and so prepare us for growth. The retired, wealthy businessman was the source of funding for the new era. Together we were going to turn the place around and be what we should be: a growing, thriving church. As I saw it, we had the resources we needed to grow into a new version of ourselves. We just needed to seize the opportunity that was before us and grow into that new identity.

It wasn't a bad vision, but as hard as I tried, I couldn't make it happen. That initial upsurge in attendance and membership was a one-time event during my seven years there. When I left the congregation at the end of seven years of service, the place looked pretty much as it had when I arrived. The faces staring back at me from the pews were older and some new old faces had joined us, but the prize of having "turned the place around" was not among the awards that I received.

Turning Toward God and the Congregation

Yet this was a turning point for me. It took a while, but after an initial period of being angry and cynical and morose (see chapter one), I realized that this moment was God's invitation to me to turn around. It was the invitation to set aside my vision and to start waking up to God and to the congregation to which God had called me to be a pastor.

At that point I realized that I had a choice. I could either turn my back on this congregation, get out quickly, and look for a place where the people were more receptive to my vision, or I could turn around, face the congregation, and begin to watch for what God might be up to in the lives of those of us who found ourselves thrown together on the corner of Rosemead and California for such a time as this.

As I look back on the challenges faced by this congregation I served in the late 1980s and early 1990s, it is clear that its plight was the plight of many churches in the country. In fact, within a five-mile radius of that church were seven other Presbyterian churches, and most of them were in the same state of decline. Five of these eight congregations had under two hundred members. We were planted or grew substantially in the post–World War II era. We had hit our attendance peaks in the late 1960s. We were in the process of burying many of our charter members. We occupied buildings that were paid for and venerated by the elderly congregants, some of whom had pounded some of the nails. So as we looked toward the future we found ourselves primarily using phrases like *congregational redevelopment* to define the essence of our ministry.

We assumed that people were in the market for a church and it was our job to sufficiently change the culture of existing congregations to make them more appealing to the church shoppers of the new day. It's clear to me now that we were aiming at the wrong target. Yet it was the target that seemed the most obvious to us, given the organizational assumptions that were a part of our foundational DNA. These were churches built in response to a cultural phenomenon taking place in the 1950s. Many of the retired pastors who now occupied the retirement home a mile away from us were a part of this mid-twentieth-century, post-war church boom. They marched into suburbs, occupied the land purchased for them by the presbytery and proceeded to develop growing concerns that were ready to meet the market demand. Going to church was a good idea back then. It was an accepted norm, and these congregations grew almost effortlessly in response to this favorable market demand.

So we set out on the quest to change the congregational culture. Fueled by the relatively new science of looking at the church through the lenses of sociology, anthropology and psychology, we led our congregations in mission studies and visioning sessions. We listened to George Barna's warnings about how the church was an example of the proverbial frog slowly boiling to death in the kettle; we paid attention to Donald McGavern's principles of church growth, especially noting how homogenous groups of people facilitate growth; we dutifully administered spiritual gifts questionnaires that were all the rage and used their results as a key to "deploying our people" for the work of the church. We talked about the new vernacular in which we needed to present the gospel. We found in Jesus' words about the new wineskins a justification for changes in styles of worship and the shape of our life together (Lk 5:37-39).

Yet, if the truth be told, our congregations merely tolerated us as we invited them to be a part of this new thing. They played along, but in retrospect I now realize that their desire to grow had not so much to do with the vision we were laying out as with a desire to bring in people who would continue the church as they knew it. The question fueling their participation in the new thing was not "How can we bequeath our church to the next generation?" It was more like "Who can we find to moderate the women's association?"

So it wasn't just me who had a vision. And though these visions were quite different from one another, they shared one trait. Neither one was really big enough to carry the day.

Neither one was bigger than what we could ask for or imagine. Neither one was really about the kingdom of God. They were both merely about building a church.

I suppose one could do studies to determine when the shift was made, but I often find myself asking the question of when and why we pastors began to believe that our primary calling was to build the church. How did we come to believe that the people we encounter are primarily in the market for a church? How did we forget that they are probably more in the market for an experience of, and ultimately an ongoing relationship with, the living God?

Beyond Strategy

In the years since my time in Pasadena, I don't hear as many people talking about congregational redevelopment. I suppose this is true for some of the same reasons that marriage and family counselors have stopped talking about achieving the goal of creating a "blended family" in the wake of divorce and remarriage. We've had enough experience with failed attempts at redevelopment that we've stopped expecting it to happen. Now the planting of new congregations is the ascendant idea for renewal.

Furthermore, the vernacular of business has joined the languages of sociology, anthropology and psychology in the discussion of church renewal. I find myself spending more time in meetings where we are using phrases like "strategic initiatives" and where we are working on "aligning our resources with our missional objectives." As is true in the realm of business, concerns about leadership, strategic planning and branding also now prominently figure into the equation of what will advance the cause of the church.

I suppose all of these disciplines have something to teach us. They give us a window into culture and our place in it. But none of them ultimately tell us about what is at the root of ministry. They can inform the way we conduct some of the activities of congregational ministry, but they do little or nothing to foster a reason for doing ministry itself.

There is nothing wrong with pastors and congregations having a vision statement or making use of organizational theory to assess the various ways we plan and lead. If we are going to ask questions about the success or survival of the church in a post-Christian culture we will no doubt need to make use of the tools of organizational analysis and leadership theory.[1] However, these things have to be informed by something bigger than themselves. They have to be informed by God's call. And God's call is always about something bigger than our plans. What God invites us to do is what informs matters like vision and leadership. There are some big words like *justice*, *righteousness*, *mercy* and *love* that give us a sense of the greater vision of God. And it is to a ministry characterized by these words that God is calling us.

A Change of Heart

As I look at the historic context of the ministry of John the Baptist, it is clear that John, like most of the Old Testament prophets before him, faced religious institutions that were in desperate need of renewal. Second Temple Judaism was in a place not unlike the corrupt ecclesiastical worlds of Hosea,

---

[1]See Scott Cormode, *Making Spiritual Sense* (Nashville: Abingdon Press, 2006) for a good discussion making use of the disciplines of leadership theory and organizational development in the context of ministry. Scott has done a good job of showing how these disciplines can serve the greater end of ministry rather than being ends in themselves.

Isaiah and Jeremiah. Thus John's message was similar to that of his prophetic predecessors. His was a message that wasn't so much about changing an institution as it was about changing human hearts.

While the message alluded to institutional foibles and lapses associated with the practice of ritual purification in the temple, it didn't primarily call for the reform of these practices so much as it called for people to engage these practices with integrity. John, like the writer of Deuteronomy, was calling for a circumcision of people's hearts (see Deut 10:16; 30:6). He was inviting them beyond a superficial religion that was built on little more than the regular dispensing of liturgical and sacramental anesthetics. He was calling them to turn around and face God.

John had plenty of reasons to invest time and energy in the rooting out of corruption and seeking institutional reform. Certainly a better organization and system could be built. There was room for proposing a new movement and a new practice of the faith. But this is not the road he took. He did not create a new movement around himself. He did not call people to reject temple practices and follow a new way. He did not build a retreat center or ashram in the wilderness by the Jordan. According to recent historic scholarship, he did not join the Essenes in their community of separation as a means of insulation from corruption.[2] In short, his calling was not primarily one of institutional reform. If that was going to happen, it was going to be a byproduct or result of

---

[2]See Joan E. Taylor, *The Immerser: John the Baptist Within Second Temple Judaism* (Grand Rapids: Eerdmans, 1997). In chapter one, Taylor debunks the connection some have made between John and the Qumran community. Her work does a good job in placing John firmly in the tradition of the Old Testament prophets.

people's cleansed and transformed hearts.

There is obviously some gold to be mined here. John's example can give us good direction in answering the question about God's call to us as pastors. The prophetic tradition points us in a direction where we see our call not in terms of running the institutions we lead, but in terms of inviting people to wake up to God. If we look at the call narratives for Isaiah and Jeremiah, it doesn't take long to see that institutional reform is not the thing that is primarily on God's mind. What is on God's mind is that the people who had fallen asleep might have a messenger who would invite them to wake up out of their religious slumber and pay attention to the truth that the living God was in their midst.

In the cases of both Isaiah and Jeremiah, we aren't given much hope that the institutions are going to change any time soon; in fact, God essentially says not to waste time with them. Rather the substance of the prophetic task is simply to invite people to turn their hearts toward God. Prophets, like John, "turn many people of . . . Israel to the Lord their God" and "make ready a people prepared for the Lord" (Lk 1:16, 17).

God's Presence in the Mess

What this tells me is that rather than spending the lion's share of our time trying to clean up the house to get it ready for renewal, we probably ought to give ourselves more fully to the work of looking for the ways in which God is showing up in spite of the mess. And just maybe, when people start to see that God is showing up, the institutions they manage will start to reflect the truth that he is present. In short, our work is to look for and give witness to these sublime divine appearances that can happen even in the seemingly mundane and maybe even broken contexts of average congregations.

John the Baptist's story gives witness to this principle in an encounter between John's father, Zechariah, and Gabriel, a messenger from God. Luke does a masterful job of storytelling throughout his Gospel, but here at the beginning I especially love the way he mixes the mundane and sublime. Zechariah is just doing his job when he is encountered by the angel Gabriel. As a temple priest, it was his turn to go in and offer the incense offering. His "section was on duty" (Lk 1:8), and his number came up to preside at this service.

On the one hand, this is a story about the unique privilege of entering the Holy Place and administering a rite that one seldom got to administer. With twenty-four units of Aaronic priests, comprising about eighteen thousand priests in all, it wasn't very often, and perhaps only once in his life, that Zechariah got the chance to preside at the altar of incense. Yet it was a rite that happened twice daily at the temple, once before the morning burnt offering and once after the evening burnt offering. Like all priests, Zechariah was in a unique place to handle holy things. Yet like all priests, he no doubt faced the liability of allowing the holy to become mundane because those holy things were handled every day.

What pastor doesn't know this same tension? Our work regularly takes us into those holy places not only of proclaiming the Word and administering sacraments of the church but also of people's lives. What feels special and unique to our congregants can seem commonplace to us. Familiarity breeds a kind of easy comfort with the presence of holy things. Once in this place, our spiritual senses become dulled and we miss the divine invitations that come our way. Thus every so often God does something radical to break into our stunted imaginations with a reminder that he is very much present and at work in our midst.

Such was the case with Zechariah. At one level his is a story of mundane, commonplace religious ritual that on the surface is about as exciting as the text on the typical church's outdoor board:

Morning and Evening Incense Offering
7:00 a.m. and 7:30 p.m.
Fr. Zechariah, presiding

Yet while Zechariah is simply doing his job, he is reminded by the angel Gabriel that his job fits into a picture that is much bigger than what he normally recognized. It is not clear what Zechariah is praying for when he goes into the sanctuary to make the incense offering, but what he receives in answer to his offering is an invitation from God to be a part of his story of redemption.

To paraphrase Gabriel's words: "Zechariah, you and your wife Elizabeth will play a role in God's story that you have not imagined playing. The two of you are going to have a baby boy. God is going to dispossess you of your expectations of childlessness and alter the course you have set out for yourselves. God will bring joy into your lives and ask you to steward the life of this servant of his to whom Elizabeth will give birth. Your child will be God's prophet. Like Elijah he will continue the work of issuing God's invitation to his people. He will call them to turn toward God and to allow their covenant relationship with God to be the foundation of all of their relationships. He will point people in God's direction and invite them to expect God to be a significant part of their lives."

Zechariah was not quick to accept this alteration of his expectations. The outlandishness of the story was apparently a bit much for him to digest in that moment. His reply to Gabriel betrays a bit of skepticism: "How will I know that this is so? For I am an old man, and my wife is getting on in years" (Lk 1:18). But Gabriel seems to have little time to engage this skepticism, and before he takes his leave, he in effect tells Zechariah, "Shut up and watch."

Zechariah seems to have had little choice but to accept this invitation, and for at least the next nine months or so he is mute. It is upon the birth of his son, John, that Zechariah begins to speak again, and his confirmation of the child's name is what loosens his tongue. At that point he effectively says the same thing that Mary the mother of Jesus says to Gabriel about her own pregnancy: "Let it be with me according to your word" (Lk 1:38). Let me take up this life into which you are inviting me. Let me be a part of this thing that you are working out around me. Let me participate in this work of yours that is much bigger than me.

Our Part in the Bigger Story

We know we are called by God when we begin to see the ways in which our story fits into a bigger story. When we have the sense that we are characters in a drama that we could not write for ourselves and when we see that we are a part of something that is more than we could ask for or imagine, it is then that we begin to know ourselves as people who are called by God.

It may take us some time to realize this fact. Like Zechariah, we may need to shut up and watch for a while. But it's equally possible that we might, like Mary, hear this divine voice and be ready to marvel in the miracle of it all. Either way, when we know we are called by God, we become conscious that the everyday stuff of our lives is a part of God's story. We have a sense that we fit into a scheme that is more glorious than anything we could configure on our own.

Called into Relationship

It is interesting to me that we often use the word *call* as if a call from God is a commodity we can possess or a resource we manage and control. In this sense a call is the thing we are given to do or the task that is ours to accomplish. In my tradition we have co-opted this language of call to spiritualize what we would otherwise refer to as a job or a contract. Pastors "seek a call" when they are looking for a position in a church. We have first, second or third calls because we change churches and occupy different pulpits among different people. When we are nominated by a search committee to be the pastor of a particular congregation, we then must "negotiate the terms of the call" with the committee to settle on a salary and benefits package.

I see very little in the call narratives in Scripture that suggests there is room to negotiate terms. It seems to me the response to God's invitation is pretty much restricted to one of two answers: yes or no. The matter at hand is not about letting God know what we need to get the job done. It is about either saying yes or no to God's invitation to us to be a part of what he is doing and will do whether we acknowledge and live into our part in it or not.

Taking up the call of God can never merely be a matter of articulating and mobilizing people to carry out our vision. It isn't doing a specific job in a particular place. It is more organic than that, something more relational. To take up and act on God's call is to hear and respond to the voice of the Caller. It is to be engaged in something God gives us to be and do in the world that will draw us closer to God.

A little Latin lesson may help us here. The word *vocation* comes from the Latin *vocare*, or call. God calls out to us and we respond to his voice. God invites us into a relationship with him and thus into participation in his work. So the matter of God's call in our lives is not so much about a job description to fulfill as it is about a relationship to be engaged. It has to be about much more than carrying out a vision or strategic plan for a congregation. It is instead about taking up God's invitation to be a part of a work that was in progress long before we were ever on the scene and that will carry on long after we are gone.

Just Part of a Story

One of the things I built into my life during the years I was a pastor in Pasadena was to meet regularly with two of the other Presbyterian ministers who found themselves in congregations within that five-mile radius I mentioned above. Craig, Dan and I would get together for coffee every other week for the purpose of *supporting* one another. Actually, the more accurate way to describe our times together is that we came together to expel the venom of cynicism that had been welling up in each of us over the previous fourteen days. The primary focus of our time together was sharing the crazy stories that grew out of the thankless task of trying to get our congregations to accept and act on our visions for them.

On many days, this would consist of bemoaning the mess our predecessors had left us. In our minds, our predecessors were burned-out incompetents who had held on to their jobs too long and in so doing, delivered to us congregations on life support rather than healthy communities who were a part of God's mission in the world. As the scenario played out, we were the saviors called in by the people of our congregations to reverse the tide of this poor leadership. We were the anti-types, and thus antidotes, to our predecessors. We were new clergy for this new age in ministry. Like the man from Macedonia in Paul's dream, calling him to come over to Macedonia to help a fledgling church (Acts 16:9), these congregations had invited us to come in and help them chart a new course. And had our predecessors not left us with such a morass of trouble, we would certainly be a lot farther down the road of renewal than we currently found ourselves.

One day in the midst of such an exchange, Craig stopped us and said, "You know, I've just had a scary thought. The same people who called us to these churches also called the guys who preceded us." The poignancy of his observation wasn't lost on any of us. At first we laughed, but not too long after that laugh we also felt a bit foolish. It was a little hard to swallow the thought that we might actually share some of our predecessors' characteristics or that our congregations saw us as merely a part of their continuing narrative rather than as the heroes who would radically alter it. It was a moment of truth and a flash of light that served as a reality check for us. We hadn't come into these congregations to create a tectonic shift or radical revolution. We were just the next chapter in a story that had begun to be told before any of us were even born.

I am sure it was already clear to each of us before that day that we were probably not going to be written up in the history books as the ones who turned these congregations around through the magnitude of our faith, the strength of our perseverance or the brilliance of our vision. Yet what rang out the clearest that day was the truth that we were simply a part of a continuing story that may or may not culminate in a renewed congregation. What we were in the process of learning was that, irrespective of the accomplishment of our visions, we were going to be given the opportunity to give witness to and participate in God's story as it was being written among the members of each of our communities of faith.

3

COVENANT

Proclaiming the Good News
Versus Managing the Message

And you, child, will be called the prophet of the Most High; for you will go
before the Lord to prepare his ways, to give knowledge of salvation to
his people by the forgiveness of their sins. By the tender mercy
of our God, the dawn from on high will break upon us,
to give light to those who sit in darkness and in
the shadow of death, to guide our
feet into the way of peace.

LUKE 1:76-79

At its core, the gospel is a message about God reconciling all creation to relationship with him. It is the assertion of the truth that in Jesus Christ "all things hold together" (Col 1:17). As pastors, our prophetic role calls on us to give witness to this divine offer of covenant relationship. Thus a big part of what it means to "make ready a people prepared for God" is to announce this invitation and to resolve to make this message something that informs every aspect of our life and work as pastors.

The Message of the Covenant

When Zechariah's mute button was disengaged after the birth of John, the words that came out of his mouth gave witness to this covenant relationship. The song that he sang was not an original text or score. It was instead a composition built on overtones that had been sounding since the beginning of time. With the singing of his Benedictus, Zechariah the priest becomes a prophet and gives voice to the invitation God never ceases to issue to his people. The Benedictus delivers the primary content of the prophetic message. If we want to know what lies at the root of the word that is different from the flower that fades or the grass that withers, we would do well to become familiar with the themes of this song.

Zechariah's Benedictus first of all sings of a God who shows up. God breaks into time. God visits his people. The NRSV translates this idea in terms of the God who "has *looked favorably* on his people" and whose tender mercy "will *break* upon us" like the dawn (Lk 1:68, 78, emphasis added). God is neither distant from nor a stranger to his people but chooses to engage them through concrete acts of salvation. The language here is reminiscent of the Song of Moses in Exodus. It alludes to the poetry of the Psalms. It sings with the same power as the promise of God's coming has in Isaiah 40. It gives witness to a God who shows favor, who wants to be with his people.

Singing the Truth

As prophets, we must first of all be prepared to tell the truth about the character of God. This God is not one who is satisfied to sit in some distant corner of the heavens and occasionally tune in to his people's cries for help. This rather is the God who makes his way known to his people, the God who "reach[es] down from on high" and "[draws us] out of mighty waters" (Ps 18:16).

The message we preach about God should capture the seemingly conflicting truths about the power and the gentleness of God. Just as Isaiah 40 gives witness to the God whose appearing means both a frightful readjustment of the landscape and the reassuring offer of embrace (Is 40:1-11), our prophetic witness testifies to the Holy One who has chosen to be in our midst (Hos 11:9).

Yet God's choice to show up is not merely about presence. God's presence produces a particular outcome. He shows up in order to save. Zechariah sings a song that tells of God's action among us. It's a song about God's work to rescue, redeem and forgive us. In Zechariah's song, these three words are descriptive of the salvation that God effects. The notions of God's work of rescuing his people from their enemies and redeeming them from slavery are images that hearken back to the Exodus. This is classic salvation language. God is our Savior. He is the one who shows mercy. He is the one who hears the people's cries for freedom and effects their release. Zechariah sings of a God who keeps his promise to sustain relationship with his people and who therefore removes the barriers to this relationship (Lk 1:72-73).

Yet the enemy to be defeated and from whom we need to be rescued is not merely a national political entity that imprisons and enslaves us. The salvation to be effected is not simply freedom from Egypt or Babylon or Rome. The enemy God overthrows is much more insidious and powerful than an empire that will eventually crumble. The oppressor who must be vanquished lays claim to the territory of the human heart. The enemy is our failure to trust God and our attempt to be gods, and this enemy is routed through the forgiveness of our sins (Lk 1:77). This God whom we have tried to crowd out pursues us and lets us know that he will not only forgive us for these attempts but also make space for us in his heart.

Here is the essence of that *good* and *comforting* news that we prophets proclaim in the deserted places of people's lives and the institutions they inhabit. We tell the truth that the wildernesses of our own making are not the last word. We point to the amazing grace of the God who has made his way to us in Jesus Christ in order to let us know that the offer of covenant relationship is still open. Prophets give witness to the truth. We point to the hard truth of humanity's attempts to find a purpose outside of this covenant for which we were created. Yet we also give witness to the liberating truth about the God who offers us a way back to covenant relationship with himself nevertheless.

Our Message

Zechariah's song sings the truth about the character and the work of God, yet it also unpacks the implications of that truth for the way we live our lives. The salvation about which the Benedictus sings is not simply the promise of a future apocalyptic event that will rout our foe. This salvation offers more than liberation; it brings with it guidance and direction. It is the "dawn from on high [that] will break upon us" (Lk 1:78), and so has the effect of giving us the light we need to see the Way on which we were created to walk. The light of God's tender mercy guides "our feet into the way of peace" (Lk 1:79).

As prophets we give witness to this light that lightens the path of life. Our work is not so much about describing the specifics of the path by proscribing the behaviors that might qualify one to walk on it. Rather we direct people's attention to the horizon and invite them to watch for the dawn of God's light. We don't tell people what to do as much as we direct their attention to the Lord who says, "Follow me." We invite them to take up God's offer of peace. For what one discovers on this path is that peace with God leads us into peace with others as well. Growing in our knowledge of God's love works itself out in acts of love toward our neighbors. To walk on the path of peace is to become an instrument of peace as well.

In short, the prophetic word is a word about covenant relationships. God has chosen to love us and invites us to love one another. The "surpassing value of knowing Christ Jesus" (Phil 3:8) as our Lord and Savior gives us a resource to share with our world. God's love poured into our hearts leads to love shared with our neighbor. Living water taken in produces springs that bubble up within us for the benefit of others (Jn 7:37-38). Here is the good news that the prophet delivers. Here is the essence of the message the church is charged to proclaim.

The Temptation of Misdirected Attention
Ministry would be so easy if it weren't for the church.

In saying this I feel a bit like Linus in Charles Schulz's cartoon *Peanuts*, who protested, "I love humanity. It's people I can't stand." Twenty-nine years in pastoral ministry has taught me over and again that the gospel and congregational ministry are at times rather strange bedfellows. The great irony of pastoral ministry among a particular congregation is that, in the midst of trying to get the word out, we spend so much time fretting over and deciding on the means of doing this that we run the risk of losing touch with the message we are seeking to proclaim.

It sounds so simple. It shouldn't be difficult to maintain a grip on this truth and allow it to be the lens through which we formulate and evaluate the ministry in which we engage. Yet we must confess it is incredibly easy for us as pastors to direct our attention to tasks and pursuits that seem disconnected from this message. The work of being a leader in the church gives credence to Jesus' observation about how the cares of the world can choke the word (Mk 4:19).

The upshot of this strange chemistry between gospel and congregational ministry is that pastors can easily slip into the mistake of confusing the work of proclamation with the work of a congregation's cultural transformation. We begin to believe that the necessary precursor to the effective preaching of the gospel is changing the culture of the place where we preach it. It seems clear enough to us in the moment. If the congregation we serve has been in decline, we conclude we need to work at reversing this trend. To do this, new people will need to come in. Yet in our hearts we know that new folks probably aren't going to be all that excited about doing church in the way this declining congregation has been doing it. Ergo, to get the word out to the people who need to hear it, we have to first make the place where they will hear it more attractive to them than it currently is.

At one level this absurd argument makes perfect sense to us. Yet the irony of this "logic" is that following it through keeps us from doing the work that is at the core of pastoral ministry. Instead of focusing our attention on how to give witness to the divine invitation of covenant relationship in that place and time, we spend our days managing the process of reworking the various media we use to communicate it. Our energy is devoted to identifying and changing "irrelevant" programs. We buy into Marshall McLuhan's assessment that the "medium is the message" and spend so much time worrying about the means by which we are giving witness to the message that we neglect the message itself. In the end the people who are present and *could* hear the message hear only the proclamation of how irrelevant their congregational culture is in the brave new world.

Not the best way to win friends and influence people.

Smashing Icons

When I arrived on the scene in Pasadena, one of the cultural icons of the congregation that I found especially irksome was the men's breakfast. For anyone who has hung around churches, I am sure the phrase "men's breakfast" conjures up all sorts of associations. This particular manifestation of a common congregational institution was a sort of cross between a meeting of the Lion's Club and an episode of Iron Chef. The mission of this group seemed to be little more than gathering monthly to "chew the fat" (both literally and figuratively). To my eyes it was ninety minutes comprised of preparing and eating large quantities of high-cholesterol foods supplemented by conversation about the Trojans, Bruins, Dodgers or Lakers.

This was not what I signed up for when I knelt for the laying on of hands at my ordination. Add to this the resentment I had about having to give up time with my family to be present at this event on a Saturday morning, and you have the equation that spurred me into action. Like a crusader on a quest for a more righteous expression of church programming, I set out to change this institution. I added a Bible study. I introduced a structured sharing time. I worked hard at engaging people in "more substantive" conversation. I was determined to move us below the surface and guide us into an exploration of deeper truths. But like the medieval crusaders, I did little to transform culture; I just caused destruction and fostered resentment.

Even though I had waited a year to initiate these reforms, I hadn't really engaged the men in any sort of process leading to this new incarnation of the program. So I shouldn't have been surprised at what happened a few months into our "new and improved" men's breakfast. One Saturday a man who had been one of the founders and organizers of the breakfast came to me before we sat down to eat and asked if he could have a few minutes before the Bible study to share something with the group.

When the time came for him to share, he passed out a sheet to all the men. At the top of the paper was the title "By-laws of the Men's Breakfast." He prefaced his reading of these bylaws with the observation, "Since we are getting so organized around here, it seems like a good time for us to adopt a set of bylaws." There were a few nervous chuckles around the room, and then he started to read.

As he read, I imagine that I looked like a cartoon character whose temperature was rising. I could feel the red heat moving up from my toes through my body and into my face. The bylaws were written in a mock "legalese" and essentially put forward a mission statement that was about exactly what I had sought to change. It was playful in its tone, but its message was clear: "Stop messing with our breakfast."

The gauntlet had been thrown down and I was going to need to respond. I suppose I had some options at this point about how to respond. Unfortunately, Jesus' message about turning the other cheek was not at the front of my mind and nothing but an angry response seemed available to me in that moment. I played the shame card. We pastors can be particularly good at playing this one. The power of our office can invest us with the abusive authority to wield the wand of spiritual guilt. Time has of course robbed me of an exact memory of what I said. But I imagine I said something like, "Well, if this is what you want this breakfast to be about, I suppose you can have it. But this *is* a church, after all, and it seems to me we ought to at least mention God at some point during our gathering. But if you don't want this, then maybe you don't need me here. I could be home with my family right now, and maybe that's the better place to be."

We didn't get to the Bible study that day. What's more, while this exchange didn't immediately kill the breakfast, I have vague memories that it at least inflicted a mortal wound; sometime over the next series of months it stopped being a regular part of the church calendar.

Some may read this story and say, "Good riddance. It needed to die." At one level, they are right. Yet the rightness of that comment begs another question: Whose job is it to smash these congregational icons? Is it anyone's job to destroy them? Or do people simply walk away from antiquated institutions as times change or as they grow in the knowledge that God is inviting them to be a part of something much bigger than the programs of a particular congregation?

A Better Way

As I look back on this experience, I find myself wishing I had responded to the men's breakfast more like Paul responded to the things that irked him about Athens (see Acts 17:16-34). He ascribed a more developed spiritual meaning to one of the everyday religious fixtures that people passed by if their path happened to take them through the Areopagus. He pointed to one religious fixture and used it as a way to give witness to a truth they had not considered. I imagine at some level, some of the men at the breakfast saw me as a "babbler" and "proclaimer of foreign divinities" (Acts 17:18). I imagine they wondered why in the world I would need to stand against what was to them a harmless congregational icon.

There was another choice to be made that day, and it was more like the choice Paul made. It was the choice to bring spiritual meaning to a practice that had lost touch with it. Paul saw the idolatry of Athens and said, "I see how extremely religious you are in every way." He saw through the inadequacy of their religion to the hunger that was behind it and spoke to the hunger and not just to the bad theology. In effect he said, "Let me give a new name to help you think differently about what you practice without thinking about it. Let me tell you about this God for whom you have no name."

There were things about the breakfast that could have given me windows into proclaiming the gospel. I didn't need to change the breakfast or get rid of it to preach with integrity. Relationship, presence and faithfulness were all potential hooks for linking the breakfast with the truths of God's kingdom. What needed affirmation was that these men wanted to be with one another and had together been members of a congregation that was an important part of their lives. There was an opportunity to proclaim the message and bring spiritual meaning to this institutional icon. I had failed to understand that the message was bigger than the medium.

Our Main Job: Proclamation

Our job as pastors is not to be the effectors of transformation as much as it is to be proclaimers of the message of the God who is in the business of transformation. While it is true that we have to do this work in places that are in various states of receptivity to the message, we would do well to recognize that the point of our work is primarily to *give witness to* the truth that leads to transformation.

At some level, all congregational ministry is cross-cultural ministry. We are proclaiming the mystery of the kingdom of God in the midst of a world that spends most of its time tuned into the reality of a very different kingdom. But in this work, our first line of attack can't simply be to lash out at that culture and publicly smash its icons. We must instead allow the gospel to do its work among the people whom we are called to serve. We must give witness to the links between their world and the kingdom of God. We must demonstrate the ways in which their story is set in the bigger context of God's story.

I suppose to some the leaps between the men's breakfast, Paul's encounter with the Athenians on Mars Hill and Zechariah's Benedictus may seem to span distances that are too big to cross. Yet I believe that these stories can teach us about the essential content of pastoral work. They all teach us that a big part of what a pastor does is to help people set their everyday stories into the context of God's big story of cove-

nant relationship with us. Prophets do the work of helping
people look at their lives through the lens of God's covenant
love. We call people to wake up to God's presence and lead
them in the work of reflecting on what difference that presence makes. We give witness to who God is and what God
has done. We also help people know how these big truths
about God intersect with their daily lives.

In short, we call people to wake up to the big context in
which their lives are set. In this way, prophets "go before the
Lord to prepare his ways." We "give knowledge of salvation"
to God's people, and we declare how the dawning of that
light both dispels the darkness of bondage and guides God's
people in the "way of peace" (Lk 1:76-77, 79).

The Trouble with Marketing and Managing

It really is *good news*. Yet we have to admit that its goodness
can become somewhat muted for us amid the details of planting, administering or trying to renew a congregation. When
most of our energy seems consumed with the question of
how we will proclaim or by what vehicles we will deliver this
message, we lose our way. Our concerns begin to center on
the abstraction of who isn't before us and who might be,
rather than identifying who is in front of us and how God
might be at work.

We place our work in the context of the marketplace and
see ourselves as competitors for people's attention. We give
our time to looking for vehicles that attract the people we
need to reach, and all the while there is something going
on right in front of us that we are neglecting. The upshot of
all this is that we stop focusing on the job of preparing
people for an encounter with God and give ourselves

mainly to the work of tweaking the delivery systems that we use to issue the invitation. Our worries start to concern themselves with matters of how well our message competes with the other retailers who are vying for their portion of the market share.

Now, in saying this, I am not suggesting that we should give no thought to those delivery systems or that we should never challenge the ineptness of antiquated congregational programs. Clearly, for prophets to be effective they must be observers of what grabs people's attention and what institutional icons are muting people's experience of God. As we will see in Luke 3, John's message to the people of his day was intentionally delivered and did not shy away from challenging the religious practices that anesthetized people to the reality of God's presence. Where we go wrong as pastors is not that we are thinking about these things but that we are thinking about them with the wrong goal in mind.

When we come to believe that our primary task is to build or save congregations, it is easy to slip out of the place where we sound like prophets and into the place where most of what comes out of our mouths sounds like what might be said in a creative meeting at an advertising agency. If our focus is merely the attempt to get people to "buy" our church, then I submit we are directing people's attention to a product rather than to a relationship with the living God.

The body of Christ is not made up of people who have merely bought into a particular church. It is made up of followers of Jesus who have responded to an invitation to relationship, and a communion of people who have made this decision looks very different from a collection of people who have decided to buy the same product.

Obviously, we need congregations to embody and contain this communion of Jesus' followers. Furthermore, as pastors we have to give a great deal of energy to thinking about and adjusting the programs of these congregational containers. Yet if these earthen vessels that hold the precious contents of the gathered community become an end in themselves, we will probably stop being prophets and begin to weight our work more heavily in the realm of management and sales. Once we enter this realm, our work is powered mainly by observations concerning who isn't in our congregation and what we might be doing to get them there. We call this evangelism, yet as we do this work, we actually stop preaching the good news to those who are right in front of us. Instead of paying attention to the work of God in our midst and giving witness to that work, we are lost in the dreams of what might be if only our calcified and immovable congregants would just grab a hold of our vision.

Holy Indifference

There is a more fulfilling choice to make. It's the choice to live in the present and look for the signs of God's work in that moment. To do this requires us to look at those irksome things about our congregations through the lenses of what the Ignatian fathers and mothers refer to as "holy indifference." It requires us to hold onto the truth that God's love and God's work among us will always be bigger than our feeble attempts to give witness to them.

A holy indifference to our plans and programs enables us to hold on to them loosely and to live in the security of knowing that God is at work in ways that are far superior to our plans. It doesn't keep us from planning but enables us to live in the moment, laugh at ourselves and not fret too much over the difficulties of surmounting those perceived barriers to ministry. When we are cringing over matters of the medium, a shot of holy indifference can redirect our attention to the grandeur of the message.

The sanctuary of the church in Pasadena had been built in the early 1960s. It was a well-built structure that reflected the modern architecture of that period. The building design was the typical A-frame so popular then. It didn't really have a steeple but something that looked more like a spire, and at the top of this was a stylized Celtic cross.

At one point during my tenure, a powerful windstorm bent the cross to the place where it was at almost a perfect right angle to the spire. A couple of days after the damage was done, Don, our elder chairperson of buildings and grounds, came to me with an idea of how to fix it. He told me about a handyman who, seeing the damage, had offered his services to repair it by cutting off the cross at the place of the bend and then reaffixing it to the spire with U-clamps. As I recall, what was most attractive about this plan to Don was the price. The handyman was going to do the whole job in one day for two hundred dollars. Don was so excited to get this off his plate that he offered to pay it himself.

I was, to say the least, not excited by this solution. Yet, to be honest, I had little or no energy to enter into a discussion about it or lead a process to figure out how to fix it. Perhaps I was still recovering from the leak in the roof over the organ pipes. So I told Don to do what he felt was best.

The day our handyman showed up, I immediately began to regret my decision. He was a man well into his sixties with a smile on his face and alcohol on his breath. In discussing the job with him, I found out he was not intending to use a crane but to climb the spire using gear something like what a lineman might use to climb a telephone pole. This was seeming to be an increasingly bad idea with every piece of information I acquired, proving the judgment of the preacher in Ecclesiastes that with increasing knowledge comes increasing sorrow (Eccles 1:18). Yet even so, I made the decision to continue to endorse Don's plan. I decided, however, the best course of action for me was not to watch. In fatigue, I succumbed to indifference, but it was far from holy. Visions of Laurel and Hardy moving a piano came to mind, and I decided to seek my bliss in ignorance.

At the end of the day, I walked out front to survey what I hoped would be a completed job. I hadn't heard any sirens during the day, so I knew that our worker had not fallen. I looked up and was met with a result even uglier than I'd expected. The cross was noticeably shorter. The use of the U-clamps meant that much of the unbent area of the upright had been needed to affix the cross securely to the spire. The U-clamps were chrome and huge. In addition, the cross was facing in a different direction. Prior to the storm, it could be seen by people as they traveled up and down Rosemead Boulevard. Now, instead of being perpendicular to Rosemead, it was parallel to it and so it appeared from a distance to look more like a lightning rod than a cross.

This was clearly not the way I wanted to communicate with our community about who we were and what we were about. The repair stuck out like a sore thumb with a huge bandage on it. The violence it did to the aesthetics and design of the building cried out with the message that we cared very little about the way we looked. Yet beyond all of this, the outcome of the repair was that from the perspective of a driver approaching us from either the north or the south on Rosemead Boulevard, it would not have been unreasonable to conclude that we were Mormons.

I never said a thing about that repair until now, and over the years I have come to value this decision. I have also come to value the image of that asymmetrical, disproportionate cross that was hastily reaffixed to our building. It stands for me as a testimony to the truth that the message of the gospel is bigger than the medium through which we present it. This seemingly tacky fixture on top of our building was a poignant depiction of both the character of our congregation and the power of the message we proclaimed. It told the truth that we were kind of bolting things together and muddling through by the grace of God. It also proclaimed what Paul declared to the sophisticated Corinthians when he pointed to God's decision to save the world through the foolishness of the cross (1 Cor 1:21).

On Madison Avenue, the work of managing the message becomes almost more important than the message itself. Tapping into—or even manipulating—people's desires to get them to buy what they haven't bought is the work of advertising. The focus is on creating a reality or fostering a hunger. It shall not be so with us (to paraphrase Jesus' words in another context). For us, the message is far more important than the medium by which it is delivered. What's more, we can rest in the truth that this message will endure irrespective of our attempts to make it more relevant or our failure to give attention to the package in which we present it.

Zechariah's Benedictus summarizes both the content and the effect of our work. Prophets give witness. Prophets make ready a people. Prophets invite people to pay attention to the presence and work of God. When this seed we sow takes root, when this ray of light we reflect dispels darkness, a big part of our work in people's lives is done. Our job is not to take responsibility to direct the steps of people's paths but to entrust them to the God who will guide them in the way of peace.

4

COMMISSION

Accepting Our Office
Versus Cultivating Loyalty

Then Jesus came from Galilee to John at the Jordan, to be baptized by him.
John would have prevented him, saying, "I need to be baptized by you, and do
you come to me?" But Jesus answered him, "Let it be so now; for it is proper for
us in this way to fulfill all righteousness." Then he consented. And when
Jesus had been baptized, just as he came up from the water, suddenly
the heavens were opened to him and he saw the Spirit of God
descending like a dove and alighting on him. And a voice
from heaven said, "This is my Son, the Beloved,
with whom I am well pleased."

MATTHEW 3:13-17

One night while at a church dinner in one of my seminary internship congregations, I found myself seated next to one of the elders. Phil was a large man with a large presence in the church. He was clearly among the "majority stockholders" of this particular congregation. At one point during the meal, he took the opportunity to round out my training with a bit of unsolicited wisdom. He told me that whenever the congregation got a new pastor, he would find a moment early in that pastor's tenure to take the pastor aside and give a particular speech. It went something like this: "This is my church. I was here before you got here. I'll be here after you leave."

I do not know how this ritual "shot across the bow" had been received by the pastors who were its target. It was somewhat of a power play and thus could either instill fear or invite a challenge from the one at whom it was aimed. Yet there is a part of me that appreciates the ring of truth in this warning shot. In effect Phil was saying, "Don't mess with our church. Just be our pastor. We are more than a listing on your resume or an object of your leadership. We're a congregation that was here before you got here and we'll probably be around after you leave. So be who we've asked you to be and we'll get along great."

What I like about Phil's warning is that it reminds pastors to respect the boundaries of the office we are called to occupy. As pastors we are often too quick to use first-person possessive pronouns when speaking about the congregations we serve. The congregations in which we work are not ours. Rather we occupy a post that we inherit from our predecessor and pass on to our successor. The story of a congregation is always bigger than the recounting of its succession of pastors.

Yet at another level Phil's speech to his pastors was somewhat disingenuous. For if pressed on this, I am sure he would have had to admit that he expected far more from his pastor than his statement implied. Had I had the benefit of age and experience that would have emboldened me to pursue the discussion, the superficiality of his warning would have emerged. I know that he would have had to admit that he needed much more from his pastor than to marry, bury, preach and pray. He would have expected his pastor to be both the chief steward of his congregation's resources and its loving shepherd. He needed not just a religious functionary to "say the words" or to administer the affairs of the congregation, but a sister or brother in Christ who would help him wake up to the presence of God. Phil no doubt expected his pastor both to preside objectively over the business of the congregation and to shed a tear when standing next to an open grave.

Our Role in an Existing Community

Part of what it means to be a pastor is to be commissioned to an office. It is to be invited by people to perform a specific task and occupy a particular post. This task we perform could be carried out by others. This post we occupy could be filled by others. "For such a time as this" we find ourselves in a particular place among a particular people doing the things our office commissions us to do.

Yet the confounding reality that confronts us as we perform these duties is that they usher us into personal spaces. The people who invite us there don't merely want us to provide them with an ecclesiastical service; they want us to bring all of who we are to that moment of ministry and be fully present as we give witness to the presence of God. The result of this is that it becomes very easy for us, and for the members of our congregations, to confuse our office with our person. It's an easy mistake to make. To enter the life of a congregation is to enter the world of a people with an ongoing history. We get caught up in a web of relationships that pre-dates us and will continue after us. We spend a good bit of our time growing to know and letting ourselves be known by these people. Yet we will never be a part of them in the same way that they are a part of one another.

More than once I have found myself marveling at the way the title "pastor" grants me access to situations and places where I would not have otherwise been invited. Over the years I have found myself in venues as diverse as occupying a place on the dais, praying the invocation during a political party gala at the Century Plaza Hotel in Los Angeles and standing just outside a delivery room in the obstetrics department at the University of Washington Medical Center, waiting for a mother to give birth to twin daughters, one of whom she knew was about to die. In both cases I was there to pray and give witness to God. It was both my office and my relationship with the people involved that occasioned the invitation into these spaces. In these places of privilege, I am almost always tempted to believe that my parishioners need *me* to be there, yet who they actually need is their pastor. At that moment I have a job to do, a role to perform, yet in that moment it is *me* doing that job and performing that role.

A Job and a Relationship

So how do we draw this ambiguous line between our person and our office? How do we remain cognizant of the tension between these two identities? If we make the job too much about us, then our work is characterized by winning friends and influencing people. Yet if we move too far in the opposite direction, we run the risk of a kind of professional disengagement that does little to build relationship with the people among whom we serve.

Paul's rhetorical question in 2 Corinthians comes to mind,

"Who is sufficient for these things?" (2 Cor 2:16). How do we bring ourselves fully into genuine relationship with the people of the congregations we serve and yet never lose sight of the truth that we are not, and never will be, merely members of these congregations? There are expectations placed on us that we be passionate and yet also totally objective; that we be close enough to be available when needed yet not so close that we stick our noses in places where folks don't want them; that we live exemplary Christian lives yet not be so holy that we are unapproachable. Who indeed is sufficient for these things?

Paul's rejoinder to this question gives us some insight in approaching an answer. He goes on to say, "For we are not peddlers of God's word like so many; but in Christ we speak as persons of sincerity, as persons sent from God and standing in his presence" (2 Cor 2:17). Coming from God, we stand in the presence of God and give witness to God. We have no commodity to sell, no point to prove, no favor to earn; our work is to bring ourselves fully and sincerely to the task of giving witness to God. In other words, the work is not about us; it is about our paying attention to God's work and bringing ourselves fully to that work.

Paul's struggle with the Corinthian congregation is indicative of what every pastor faces as we navigate the line between our office and our person. Our office calls on us to the simple act of giving off the scent of Jesus (2 Cor 2:15-16) as we live among a particular people at a particular time. In the course of going about this work, there will be times when the smell of Jesus makes people mad and times when their response to this scent bears the fruit of gratitude and approval. Yet the bearers of these emotions usually do not direct these

affections to God, but to us. The scent of Jesus can be con-
fused with the scent of the pastor, and suddenly we become
the recipient of things that do not belong to us.

Pastor as Pretender

The people in our congregations rarely distinguish between
our office and our person. They rarely see us merely as mes-
sengers of God. They do not primarily see us as ones who
function in an iconic way, that is, as people whose job is to
direct their attention to God. Thus one of the unavoidable
hazards of ministry is that we become a target for their projections. The business they have to do with God will sometimes pass through us on its way to God. This feels good
when we are being congratulated for our insight or thanked
for our presence. Yet it stabs us with pain when we are being
castigated for our apparent unresponsiveness or upbraided
for our failures to come through for people in the way they
expected.

In our saner moments, we know that we are never as good
or as bad as people in our congregations might see us. Yet
that sanity is not always readily accessible to us, and we occasionally fall prey to those insecure moments when we
allow the approval and disdain of our congregations to define us. When this happens, our goal in ministry degrades
into making people happy or avoiding their wrath. Like
pagan priests, our primary ministry becomes making sacri-
fices to the gods of our congregation that either beseech their
approval or divert their anger.

At this moment we stop faithfully performing our office
and we stop being true to our person. We instead take up the
role of a pretender. Donning a mantle that could be called

our pastoral persona, we start to fake it. This persona that we develop strives primarily to earn the loyalty and approval of members of the congregation. We want people not only to feel good, but to feel good about us. So we create a pastoral façade. We start to hide from the call of God because it feels safer to fake it than to be available to be a part of the work that is bigger than ourselves.

A few years ago, when my daughter was about fifteen, we drove to church together one morning. As we got out of the car and began to walk toward the building, she caught my attention and with a smile on her face said, "There it is." I replied, "What?" And she said, "Your pastor smile." This wasn't the first time an observation like this had been made about me by my family. The walk from the parking lot to the sanctuary is its own kind of metamorphosis. Like Superman shedding his clothes to reveal his superhero suit underneath, I get out of the car and don my pastor smile. It's show time—time to kick my extrovert into gear and greet the congregation.

My daughter's observation is what C. S. Lewis called "a severe mercy." It both pokes me with the truth of my duplicity and invites me to a place of integrity. It reminds me that I am a real person who occupies an office. That morning in particular, the smile seemed to her to be more a part of the costume of a persona than a reflection of a real person, and it was helpful to me to be reminded of the easy descent to that place. It was good to be known in that moment and called back to reality. There is freedom in being awakened from the fictional world of the pastoral persona and delivered into the real world of a real person who happens to hold a pastoral office. There is good news in noticing that we have just tripped over ourselves.

In those moments when we have been reminded of this hazard, we need to keep in mind a simple truth. To quote Paul once again, we need to be aware that "it is by God's mercy that we are engaged in this ministry" (2 Cor 4:1). This means re-rooting ourselves in the reality that in and of ourselves we are neither qualified for nor excluded from the work to which we have been called. Neither our positive accomplishments nor our personal failings are the primary arbiter in determining the matter of our sufficiency for the work. What is more at issue is the extent to which we see ourselves as gratefully receiving God's merciful invitation to participate in his work. When we understand ourselves primarily as people who are called by God to participate in a work that is bigger than the work we initiate, we will be able to relegate both the gratitude and the criticisms of our congregations to a place that weakens their demand for attention.

Working Beyond Our Adequacies

Our office takes us into places where we would not otherwise be permitted to go and where we might not venture if we had nothing but our own skills or pedigree to sustain us. Navigating the tension this truth produces is one of the disciplines of pastoral ministry. Therefore, in those moments when we know beyond any doubt we are not qualified in and of ourselves to rise to the occasion of the ministry set before us, we need to look for some assurance that the call of God is what both beckons us into and sustains us in that place.

The story of Jesus' baptism is an example of John's interaction with this dynamic. Called by God to be that voice in the wilderness, giving witness to sin, inviting people to repentance and offering them an invitation to take up the path of righteousness, John was clear on what business he was to be about. Gabriel's eloquent description of his office had probably been relayed to John by his father, Zechariah, more than once. Furthermore, once John began acting on this call and performing the duties of his office, it probably became clear to him both that he was good at the job and that he was participating in a work that was much bigger than him.

Of the Gospel writers, Mark is the most exuberant in his description of the effect of John's faithfulness to God's call: "And people from the *whole Judean countryside and all the people of Jerusalem* were going out to [John], and were baptized by him in the river Jordan, confessing their sins" (Mk 1:5, emphasis added). Obviously John's faithfulness to his office was bearing fruit. He had a popular ministry. He struck a chord that resonated with people. The truth, though hard to hear, was good news to people, and apparently John did a good job of delivering it.

We cannot know how John received this success. No information about his internal process around this theme is available to us. But, given that John was as human as the rest of us, he probably wrestled with the tension between being a bit self-congratulatory and being a bit embarrassed by the misplaced approbation of the crowds who came out to see him.

In the moment that Jesus approaches him for baptism, this tension no doubt came to a head. By Matthew's report, "John would have prevented [Jesus], saying, 'I need to be baptized by you, and do you come to me?'" (Mt 3:14). What is clear to John in this moment is his lack of qualification for the task he is being asked to complete. His office had ushered him into a space where his person would not have been invited, and he responded to that conflict with an initial hesitancy to engage the task.

If John at that moment believed Jesus to be the Messiah, then Jesus' request was probably a bit of a stretch for him. Who was he, after all, to take on the task of baptizing the "Lamb of God who takes away the sin of the world" (Jn 1:29)? John's baptism was about calling people to repentance and inviting them to take up a new journey of righteousness. It was a sign of a decision made to turn from evil and to take up God's invitation to live out the implications of the covenant relationship. None of this seemed applicable to and appropriate for the one who was standing in front of him. Furthermore, though John's personal righteousness and example were never the sources of his preaching, comparison with Jesus in that moment brought to the fore an awareness of his relative personal inadequacy for the task of calling people to live righteously.

Yet what was at issue here was not John's adequacy for the task, and Jesus made that clear. Furthermore, in Jesus' response to John's hesitancy, we have what we need as pastors to accept our office in those situations where we are painfully aware of our personal inadequacy for a particular pastoral task: "Let it be so now; for it is proper for us in this way to fulfill all righteousness" (Mt 3:15).

In other words, "It may indeed seem inappropriate for you to do this, John. You may feel unqualified and out of place. But permit it for now. Permit it because this is a part of something bigger than *your ministry* and what you might think your ministry means. This is bigger than the question of your qualifications and adequacy for this task. It's a part of the work of God, and in this moment you are being invited to participate in that work. So do your work and let God show you how it is a part of a greater work that God is doing."

For Matthew, Mark and Luke, the baptism of Jesus seems to be an illustration of what Paul sang about in Philippians 2:1-11. Jesus' baptism is of a piece with his self-emptying act of incarnation, crucifixion and resurrection. His joining with us, identifying with our brokenness and taking on our form are all illustrated in his choice to submit to a "baptism of repentance for the forgiveness of sins" (Mk 1:4). Thus in that moment John wasn't so much carrying out "his" ministry as he was participating in the work of God. He was being invited into, and caught up in, a mystery that was way beyond anything he might have been able to conceive.

"Let it be so now." I think these words can be Jesus' guidance to us regarding how to navigate the tension of the sometimes conflicting worlds of person and office. Our office calls on us to do the work of consolation, *paraklēsis*. We are doing our job when we are coming alongside others for the purpose of giving witness to the work of God. We are fully engaged as pastors when we are issuing the invitation to look for the presence of God. When this work takes us into places that seem too big for us, we can hear in Jesus' words the call to faithfully fulfill our office and humbly acknowledge that something may be going on in that moment that is much bigger than what we might conceive. To hear the words "Let it be so now" is to hear the comforting reminder that in God's scheme of things there is always something bigger going on than what we can ask for or even imagine.

These words also call us back into reality when we fall prey to the other temptation of thinking that our own innate wonderfulness is what is fueling our ministry. They remind us that those insights about Scripture we deliver and the helpful advice we offer are merely ingredients in a divine recipe for righteousness. The One who began a good work in the people among whom we serve is in the process of completing it, and our work is part of what he is using to accomplish that end (Phil 1:6).

Understanding and being faithful to the prophetic aspect of our office helps us remember that we are not essential to the completion of God's task, but that we have been invited by God to participate in his work. Our job is to give witness to God's work, not to accomplish it on his behalf. Our competence and confidence for ministry grow out of our grateful receipt of God's merciful invitation to join him in the work he is completing. When we understand and hold onto this truth, we are liberated from both the paralyzing fear of inadequacy and the blinding arrogance of hubris. Again, to quote Paul,

> Such is the confidence that we have through Christ toward God. Not that we are competent of ourselves to claim anything as coming from us; our competence is from God, who has made us competent to be ministers of a new covenant. . . . By the open statement of the truth we commend ourselves to the conscience of everyone in the sight of God. . . . For we do not proclaim ourselves; we proclaim Jesus Christ as Lord and ourselves as your [the Corinthian church's] slaves for Jesus' sake. (2 Cor 3:4-6; 4:2, 5)

To handle holy things is a heady experience. Yet it helps to mitigate the hazard of this if we remember that our job is not to mediate or to dole out portions of this holiness to the members of our congregations. Rather we are to give witness to it and then step out of the way. A prophet's place is not between God and the people he or she is serving. It is rather to be among those people, sharing their lives and working in such a way as to invite awareness that God himself is among us.

Pastor as Town Crier and Midwife

I like to think of pastoral ministry in terms of two ancient service trades. The pastor serves in ways similar to the town crier and the midwife. The town crier gave witness to truths that could be readily discerned by anyone. He walked through the streets when others slept in order to both notice and let folks know what he saw. There isn't a whole lot of skill involved in being a town crier, but staying awake and giving witness are valuable services to a community. Much of a pastor's work is about staying awake and giving witness to the kingdom of God. This kingdom will make itself known whether we give witness to it or not. As pastors we do not usher in the kingdom—we point to it and allow people to respond as they may.

Similarly, the midwife does not cause births, she assists in them. Her work doesn't create life and she does not remain in the household to nurture the baby being born. At the most basic level, she catches babies. With or without her, the birth in which she is assisting is going to take place. Yet her presence is a gift to the mother and the family into which this child is being born. The key to the midwife's work is presence with and attentiveness to the mother who is delivering the child. She notices what is going on and moves in to respond in ways that assist the birth.

Pastors, like midwives, participate in a work in progress. God is bringing things to birth in the lives of the people among whom we serve. We get the privilege of catching these babies, of handling these holy births. With or without us this new life would happen, but by the mercy of God, we get to be a part of it and experience the joy of being invited by God to join him in his work.

More often than not, the most fulfilling aspects of my work as a pastor sneak up on me and take me by surprise. The greatest fulfillment comes not as the result of some program I have developed or some class I have designed and taught, but when I suddenly and unexpectedly find myself in the presence of an obvious work of God. God issues a subtle invitation to be a part of people's lives, and I get the opportunity to be present for and give witness to that work. It is as if God taps me on the shoulder and says, "Pssst. Hey, Dave, come over here for a minute. I want to show you something. I am going to give you a chance to be a part of what I am doing in this person's life."

There are countless stories that give witness to this experience of being invited into God's work. One in particular stands out. I was in my office with a young man who had come to see me about matters of vocation and the direction of his life. He was recently married, and he and his wife were expecting a child. He had a myriad of feelings about his life, responsibilities, relationships and work. He was excited about and fearful at the prospect of the birth of this first child. He wanted to rise to his responsibility, yet he was also terribly unhappy at the prospect of being locked into a job that did nothing to feed his soul.

He came to me to seek some insight and to pray. What neither of us knew when he entered my office was that God was going to move in and make himself known in very healing ways. This young man came seeking advice about how he should navigate the course of his life and what he left with was an experience of God's healing.

In the course of the hour we spent together, he told me a story about an encounter he had with his father when he was in high school. I do not remember why this story came up. I do know that the catalyst for its rise to the surface had nothing to do with any insightful or clever question from me. Yet when this story emerged from his heart, it unleashed something like a flash flood that results from a broken dam. Telling this story in that moment caused him to break down and weep in a way that I am sure he had never before wept. The floor in my office became wet with his tears.

His reaction was a surprise to both of us. While he was mainly in that Romans 8 place of "sighs too deep for words" (Rom 8:26), he was able at one point to say to me, "I don't know what's happening. In the past when I've told this story, I've laughed." He obviously wasn't laughing that day. But I like to think that God was—not out of derision, but out of the joy of lifting one of his children out of the pit of grief and setting his feet on the broad and open space of grace (Ps 18:19).

I got to catch a baby that day. I got to give witness to God's work of Life. It was so clear to me that this work had absolutely nothing to do with me, but by the mercy of God it was me who got to experience it. I no doubt both shared advice with and answered the questions of this young man that day. Yet when he left my office, we both knew the memorable part of the encounter would have little to do with my answers to his questions.

It was my office as pastor that brought him into my world that day. It was my presence as his brother in Christ and attentiveness to how God might be at work that assisted his liberating discovery. But above all, what was at issue that day was the work of God. As pastor I simply had a hand in helping him be ready to receive it.

5

CONTEXT

Inhabiting a Place Versus
Propagating a Program

*In the fifteenth year of the reign of Emperor Tiberius, when Pontius Pilate
was governor of Judea, and Herod was ruler of Galilee, and his brother Philip
ruler of the region of Ituraea and Trachonitis, and Lysanias ruler of Abilene,
during the high priesthood of Annas and Caiaphas, the word of God
came to John son of Zechariah in the wilderness.*

LUKE 3:1-2

The name of the church I served in Pasadena was Michillinda
Presbyterian Church. There was a street nearby of the same
name, but we sat on the corner of Rosemead Boulevard and
California Avenue. At first it seemed odd to me to name a
church for a street that was three blocks away. What I discovered, however, was that the church was actually named
for the property development in which it sat. Michillinda
Park was a real estate development that began to be built in
the 1920s in a narrow strip of unincorporated Los Angeles
County sandwiched between the cities of Pasadena and Ar-
cadia. The development was a little over two blocks wide east

to west and about eight blocks long north to south. Apparently the developers of this tract had some connection to the Midwest, because the name originates with a small resort community on Lake Michigan and is an amalgam of Michigan, Illinois and Indiana.

I realize these details may seem insignificant. But I mention them here because I came to learn that this little strip of land was sort of an orphan among communities with strong identities. Our address said we were a part of Pasadena, but in fact we weren't. We were set in Michillinda Park, a place named for a place that had little or no resonance in Southern California. Furthermore, people in this part of the San Gabriel Valley had strong attachments to the cities in which they lived. To the untrained eye, the collection of these cities might seem like nothing more than the northeastern portion of LA's urban sprawl. It is not always clear when you have crossed the border of one of those cities and entered another. However, if you live there you know which community you live in and, depending on the community, sometimes you make sure other people know it as well.

It bothered some of the people of Michillinda Presbyterian Church that they lacked this asset of being set in a defined community. It was often mentioned in any list of liabilities. To me as the new kid on the block, it seemed insignificant. *How could such a thing make a difference?* I thought. Here the church sat on one of the busiest corners in the area. We had well-maintained grounds and buildings. There was plenty of parking. According to all the church-growth experts, the congregation had the capital assets that contribute to optimal conditions for growth. People could see us, and if they visited we would have a place for them to park. Furthermore, it seemed to me that this lack of geographical identity might be a good thing from a theological perspective. If we weren't a congregation set in the limits of a particular city, perhaps this might focus our attention on our more important and enduring identity in Christ.

As much as I wanted to keep believing this, in time I began to agree with the members who saw this geographical context as a liability. It felt more and more to me like we were largely invisible. When people found out I was a pastor and asked where my church was, I would tell them and get quizzical looks in return. Usually those looks would be accompanied with a comment like, "Oh wow, I drive by that corner all the time and I didn't know there was a church there." At times it felt like we were set somewhere underwater in the southern end of Lake Michigan where the borders of Michigan, Illinois and Indiana meet. The only time people seemed to notice us in any appreciable way was when we had our annual rummage sale. On that day, people came in droves to buy up the bargains consisting of our members' castoffs. On the bright side, it was at least one time during the year when we needed plenty of parking.

As I began to put together the history of this place to which I had been called, two stories in particular helped shape my understanding. The first was a story about one of the founding mothers of the congregation, Alby Mowe. She was probably more responsible for establishing a church on that corner than anyone else. Alby started a Sunday school and in the early days scouted out the neighborhood looking for diapers hanging on people's clothes lines in order to invite the children of Michillinda Park to Sunday school. She knew her parish, and she worked it well as she filled the first church building, a neighborhood community center called Michillinda Hall, with the children who lived nearby.

The second insight came when I was going through old session minutes and happened upon notes from a discussion about whether and where the church ought to extend its outreach. I was amazed to learn that the congregation's governing board had at one point debated whether or not to reach out to the people of a neighborhood called Chapman Woods. The eastern boundary of this neighborhood was just across Rosemead Boulevard from the church. I was amazed that this conversation even occurred. Yet what it helped me see was the source of a deep-seated perception that the parish should be measured according to the geographic confines of its name and not necessarily seek to aspire to something much bigger than that.

I sincerely doubt that this depiction of the bounds of our parish was still consciously in place by the time I became pastor in 1987. For the simple reason that all but about four families in the church lived outside the boundaries of Michillinda Park, it would seem that this perception was not something that significantly influenced the congregation's self-image. However, I sometimes wonder how the strong pull of this early history, the institutional DNA of the place, was hanging on and influencing us without our being conscious of its effect.

Most of the people in the congregation perceived themselves to be welcoming and ready to receive anyone who wanted to stop in and have a look. Like Alby, they saw their mission primarily as faithfully ministering to their own and welcoming whoever ventured across their threshold. As a mentor once said to me, "The first tenet of the credo of most small community churches is 'We believe we are a friendly church.'" Such was true with Michillinda. They believed themselves to be a friendly church. So they were, both among themselves and to any traveler who came through their doors. Yet it was hard for many in the congregation to see how this place that they loved might also be a beacon of something much bigger than itself.

Small Stories and the Big Story

Every pastor's ministry is set in the context of a real place—a place defined by geography and history. It is a context that gives birth to real stories, about real people, set in real places. If we choose to remain ignorant of the stories that have shaped the character of this place, we do so to our detriment. Part of being a pastor is plugging into and becoming a part of that story that was in progress long before we ever appeared on the scene. However, what is also true is that we come into such places with a bigger story to tell, and if we ever forget this calling to proclaim the bigger story, we will fail in the prophetic dimensions of our work.

It is not an easy line to walk. We must honor and learn to love the people and the stories of the place to which we are called, but we must always be cognizant of our calling to awaken congregations to how the idolatries of a particular place can divert attention away from God. It is easy for long-standing members of a particular congregation to confuse their warm feelings about the place they worship with the presence of God.

When you have helped construct parts of the building, watched your kids progress through the various rooms of the education wing, dined a thousand times at potlucks held in the fellowship hall, and watched the caskets of your friends being carried in and out of the sanctuary, it's not hard to come to value the building and grow to love the place. It's also not hard to take the next step and confuse the place with God. It is easy for a church to become more rooted in its own history than in its identity as a part of the kingdom of God. Therefore the pastor as prophet has to live between these two places. To give effective witness to the kingdom, pastors must both understand the context in which our ministry is set and then, in the vernacular of that world, give witness to the eternal kingdom of which it is a part.

In this way, all pastoral ministry is cross-cultural ministry. On the one hand, pastors invite people to see themselves as citizens of the kingdom of God. Yet we do this work of giving witness in the midst of a culture that often doesn't readily recognize the existence of this kingdom. As the people in our congregations go about their lives in their neighborhoods, schools, workplaces, shopping centers and recreational venues, there is not much that is encouraging them to pay attention to how all of these places fit into the larger context of God's kingdom. The pastor's work therefore is to build bridges between these two worlds, to help people pay attention to how the presence of the kingdom of God in this world gives shape and meaning to their lives.

John's Context and Ours: The Wilderness

As a historian, Luke understood the importance of context, and he did a very good job of summarizing the levels of context in which John operated. At the beginning of what is now chapter 3 of his book, Luke identified the historical and geographical horizon for John's ministry. John's story was set in the context of the Roman Empire and Second Temple Judaism. Here, as in the first chapter of Acts, Luke moved through a series of concentric circles. In this case we move inward from the big circle of the political dominance of Rome to the religious center of Jerusalem, and as we do, we read the names of the leaders who occupied the seats of power in those worlds.

On the political horizon of John's story, we understand that it takes place when Tiberius was emperor, Pilate was governor, and Herod was tetrarch. On the religious horizon we see the high priesthoods of Annas and Caiaphas. Yet the context in which Luke was most interested is an obscure dot on a map about which none of the players in these powerful places give a second thought. The center of his set of circles in this text is an uninhabited region around the Jordan River. In that place is a light that shines brighter than the lights of these political and religious luminaries of the day.

The word of God doesn't issue forth from the contexts of Roman political power or the mouths of the religious aristocracy of Second Temple Judaism. Instead the word is given to the son of a priest, an ascetic prophet, who is delivering that word not in Rome or Jerusalem but out in the apparent emptiness of a deserted place. I love Luke's touch of irony in this text. At the end of this list of the "who's who" of the day, we reach the crescendo that tells us about the ministry of John. The word that makes a difference comes from the most unexpected of places. Unexpected, that is, only if one is unfamiliar with the ways of God.

Even a quick survey of the role of the wilderness in the Bible reveals that, in God's scheme of things, it is anything but a barren and unproductive place. It is a place rich with opportunities for encounter with the truth. It is a place where God's people are invited to wake up both to themselves and to God. In the wilderness, God's people are invited to wake up to their need. It is the place where the familiar moorings we tie up to and the crutches we use to prop us up are suddenly taken from us and we have to acknowledge how adrift and unstable our lives really are.

The wilderness is also a place of temptation. In the silence of that deserted context, what we hear first is the sound of our own voices inviting us with increased intensity to "spend [our] money for that which is not bread, and [our] labor for that which does not satisfy" (Is 55:2). The deprivation of the place tempts us to work harder at solutions to our hunger that will never fill us.

We have the opportunity to see ourselves more clearly in the wilderness, but it is also a place where we are invited to wake up to God. Because the wilderness strips us of the things we thought were essential, we are made ready to acknowledge our need and hear a voice that is not our own. In this way the wilderness becomes a place of dependence on God. In other words, having nowhere else to turn, we turn to God. Thus the wilderness can be a place of repentance that leads us to an experience of reorientation. Once we cease to be the center of our own lives and acknowledge our dependence on God, our lives become recalibrated according to the enduring truth of God.

In Scripture, the wilderness functions as a place of preparation. The forty-day and forty-year periods of sojourn in the wilderness are periods of preparation for living into a new thing that God is about to do. As God's people move from Egypt to the Promised Land, as Elijah moves from depression and despair to confidence and hope, as Jesus moves from his baptism into his ministry, they all pass through the wilderness. This in-between space is a time to encounter God and ourselves as people in relationship with God and thus to be prepared by God for the road ahead.

Call to the Wilderness

John's life and ministry was set in the wilderness, and his invitation to people was that they join him there for a while in order to come to grips with the truth about themselves and the truth about God. As I mentioned earlier, John's ministry was not one of calling people to imitate his asceticism. He was not trying to build a separatist community in the desert. Rather he adopted a very common metaphor in the story of the Jews, the wilderness, and invited his people to consider their lives in relationship to God in light of it. Furthermore, he made use of a common religious practice of the day—purification rites—in communicating his invitation to others to put their lives right before God.

Although he himself donned the mantle of Elijah and withdrew from the world, his was not a ministry of calling people to reject culture or the practices of the temple; instead John issued an admonition against allowing temple ritual to numb one to the presence of God. In short, he understood and spoke to the culture in which his ministry was set, but he also called people to set their lives in that culture in a bigger context. He invited them to come out into the wilderness to take a step back and see that their lives had everything to do with God.

The voice in the wilderness is a voice that invites people to wake up. It is a voice that, like John's, calls people into a deserted place where they can get away from the haze of their day-to-day lives that obscures the presence of God. Yet it is also a voice that greets people who are living in various wildernesses of sin and grief with the good news they need to hear.

The wildernesses we occupy are not always venues we choose. Like the wilderness wanderings of the people of Israel described in the Pentateuch and like the exile at the hands of the Babylonians, God's people often find themselves in various wildernesses as a result of their hardened hearts and refusal to acknowledge God. Like Elijah and David, God's people also find themselves having fled to the wilderness as a hideout from evil power and injustice. When we meet people in these spaces, our work as prophets is to announce that wilderness is not the last word and that God's intention for us is not defeat and deprivation but victory and abundance.

So, along with Matthew and Mark, Luke found expression for the character of John's ministry in Isaiah 40. This word of consolation to the exiles in Babylon provides the metaphor for John's work. In a world where things are askew, prophets give witness to the One who is making things right, the God who makes his way to us in order to guide our feet in the way of salvation and peace.

So whether we are inviting people to come away and get a better perspective on life or speaking into the deserted spaces of their lives, the work of the prophet often takes place in the wilderness. Prophetic work is done in an in-between space, where with one hand we grip the thread of God's hope and with the other we feel gripped by life in a world that seems to deny the very hope we profess. Prophets proclaim the

Word in the context where there is tension between confidence in the "glory about to be revealed to us" and the travail of the groaning of creation (Rom 8:18, 23). Our job is to be truthful about the latter and to never cease to give witness to the former.

If we ever stop honestly acknowledging the truth about the bad news, we will mute the power of the good news. The wilderness is where this is all held in tension. While we talk about it as if it is an aberration to the norm of our lives, it is actually a great description of our daily experience of the way of faith in Jesus. Living between the "already and not yet" of the kingdom of God, we move through the wilderness needing to know both that God is with us and that wilderness is not the last word.

Prophets Within the Congregation

Yet, unlike John, we pastors do this work in congregations. Although the prophetic seeds of the Word we sow might initially take hold and grow, they are often choked out by the cares of the world, such as the building fund of the church. Here is where we have to admit that John the Baptist as a metaphor for pastoral ministry begins to break down. This perhaps is the reason people often cast me a quizzical glance when I say I am writing a book about how John the Baptist's ministry is a paradigm for pastoral ministry today.

While John knew and spoke to the realities of his culture, he was not trying to build a going concern. Perhaps the priests of the temple raised an eyebrow at their loss of market share when people started heading out to the wilderness of the Jordan rather than through the gates of the temple to have their ritual purification needs met. Yet John had no such concern. He had very little overhead. He wasn't asking anyone for money. His invitation to wake up was not an ongoing call to support the church. It was rather a catalytic encounter designed to get people back on the right road. He was in this sense like a revival preacher called in to foster a work of renewal, but maybe not someone who would have an ongoing relationship with a particular portion of the people on the Way. The difficulty for us, of course, is that unlike John, pastors do the work of a prophet while living in and among a congregation, and this can obscure our work as prophets.

Much of what we do in a congregational setting can work against the prophetic invitation to assess life through the biblical lenses of wilderness and kingdom. Rather than being the place where we call people to focus on this bigger picture, it can become a place where we merely invite them to add another small thing to their checklist of obligations. The church as institution has worldly needs, and accumulating the resources it needs to sustain its institutional life is a full-time job. It's not just the parochial perspective of congregants that allows the mission of the church to become nothing more than sustaining itself. Pastors are just as culpable in the process of creating an institution that avoids transforming encounter with the God who called them into being in the first place. It's just too easy to confuse a commitment to fund and maintain the program and buildings of the church with the bigger work of offering our lives in service to the kingdom of God.

The Kingdom–Congregation Tension

I still remember my first sermon series at Michillinda. Four years before I arrived to be pastor, the congregation had been through a rough pastoral transition of saying goodbye to a pastor who had served there for almost twenty years. In the wake of the conflict that ensued over this separation, many people left the church. Yet this latest exodus was really nothing more than a continuation of a decline that had begun in the early 1970s. So to address this congregation that had accommodated itself to decline, I decided to preach an eight-week sermon series drawn from Isaiah 40–55, one of my favorite portions of the Old Testament. Its images of anticipating the end of exile and the beginning of God's new thing seemed the perfect metaphor to invite the folks at Michillinda to see themselves in light of something bigger than their history of decline.

Of course, at the time I thought it was a homiletic and theological tour de force. After all, who would not be inspired by the promise of the end of the exile of our decline and the invitation to join in building the highway back to the repatriated Jerusalem of a new Michillinda Presbyterian Church? Who wouldn't jump on board with this appealing vision and take up the cause of forgetting the former things and pressing on to claim the new thing we would become (Is 43:14-21)? Yet at the end of the series, the ship didn't set sail with very many crew members aboard.

The problem with the correlation between exile and Michillinda is that it made sense only to a few congregants and to me. I looked at the church's situation and saw exile and deprivation on its way to a restoration of renewal and growth; most of the congregation looked at their situation and saw a friendly church that needed to keep offering fellowship and friendliness to everyone who walked through their doors. As a friendly church, they were mainly concerned not with turning the place around and moving into a new day but with raising enough resources to sustain the former thing they had come to love. I was asking them to become workers for my vision of turning the church around, and they were asking me to help in the process of ensuring that there would be enough to keep the place going. I looked at them and saw a people who were bequeathing a legacy to a brand-new generation, and as they looked at me they saw a nice young man who would attract other nice young families to the church.

We were obviously missing one another. More importantly, we were both missing the point. By focusing primarily on a vision of a new Michillinda Presbyterian Church, we were diverting our attention from the only means by which we would ever become that new thing. The primary work before us was not the development of a strategy by which to grow or sustain the ministry of Michillinda Presbyterian Church. The real work was coming together in the task of attending to what it looks like to follow Jesus in our world. The church as institution was never meant to be an end in itself. It is not the destination of the journey of faith. Rather a congregation is a wide spot in the road where we come together for rest, encouragement and challenge. It is a real place, a context in which we live, but a context that is much, much bigger than itself, and it is in this bigger context that we are primarily to give witness.

As I close out this chapter, I'd like to briefly take us back to Michigan to tell a story told to me by one of the retired Presbyterian ministers who lived in the retirement community near the church. Paul did not attend Michillinda but would show up to worship on occasion and afterward in the patio regale me with tales about his own years of service as a parish pastor. He seemed to me to be the quintessential extrovert pastor who no doubt had circled his flock with the tireless energy of a sheepdog and managed the ways of his congregation with an air of authority and an eye for detail. Whenever Paul introduced himself, he would state his name and then tell you how he had served for over forty years as a pastor in rural congregations in Michigan. He used to tell me that he loved the name of our church. "I love the ring of it, *MICH-illinda*," he would say. In fact, it was Paul who told me about the resort community after which we were named.

On one occasion when Paul and I were talking, he found out that Michillinda was going to be hosting a meeting of the San Gabriel Presbytery and proceeded to tell a story of a time when one of his congregations in Michigan had hosted their presbytery. Apparently the presbytery didn't get out their way very often, and it was a special treat for him to be able to show off his congregation to his colleagues from other churches in the presbytery. At one point during the day, overwhelmed by the good feelings of being able to offer this hospitality, Paul marched into the kitchen where the members of the women's association were preparing lunch. In a moment of gratitude and generosity, with arms opened wide, he issued the order: "Ladies, cut the pies in sixes." As he told me this, he shot me a grin and offered the conclusion: "The presbytery never forgot it."

So, what on earth does this story have to do with anything I have been talking about?

I tell it here because it is a story about context and as such I find this story to be both quaintly appealing and a blatant invitation to respond with righteous disdain. On the one hand, I am attracted to Paul's remembrance and celebration of a real place. On the other hand, I want to push away this quaint depiction of church. While I honor how it speaks of the smells, tastes and relationships that are a part of living in a real place, it is such a small vision of the church that it repels me.

In answer to this tension, what I need to tell myself is, "Welcome to pastoral ministry." It is in the space of just this tension that we live out our pastoral lives. For the church needs at some level to be a warm and hospitable place that is a refuge from the world. It needs to be a comforting place where there are generous portions of pie. But it also needs to offer a very different kind of consolation as well. It needs to be the place not just where we minister to ourselves but where we set our lives in the context of the kingdom of the God who has chosen to minister to us and through us to the world.

Like it or not, if we choose to be prophetic pastors, we will never cease to live in the paradox of these polarities. There is no magic formula for how we do this other than remaining aware of the tension. We have no choice but to embody ministry in a place, yet we must never forget that this place belongs to a context that is much bigger than itself. If for the sake of our allegiance to the kingdom of God we ignore the realities and peculiarities of a congregation, we will never learn the vernacular that will enable us to give witness to the kingdom in that place. Or if we become so acculturated to the ways of a congregation that we begin to confuse it for the kingdom of God, we forfeit our role as prophets and become nothing but an ecclesiastical functionary in that place. Our role as prophets takes us to a space that is in between these two contexts. God help us as we seek to navigate that terrain.

6

CONFRONTATION

Inviting Awareness Versus
Administering Anesthesia

John said to the crowds that came out to be baptized by him,
"You brood of vipers! Who warned you to flee from the wrath to come?
Bear fruits worthy of repentance. Do not begin to say to yourselves, 'We have
Abraham as our ancestor'; for I tell you, God is able from these stones to raise
up children to Abraham. Even now the ax is lying at the root of the trees;
every tree therefore that does not bear good fruit is cut down and
thrown into the fire." . . . So, with many other exhortations,
he proclaimed the good news to the people.

LUKE 3:7-9, 18

As I read through the various call narratives of the biblical prophets, it seems clear that very few, if any, tell the story of a prophet who acted on his vocation as a result of his sheer love for the act of preaching. It's hard to imagine Jeremiah saying, "I have a passion for preaching and that's why I'm willing to take all this abuse." Instead, what we find in both the Old and New Testaments is the description of a group of people who would rather have been doing anything but preaching, yet found themselves in those figurative and literal pulpits because they couldn't dodge the call of God.

The nobility of their calling is impressive and makes me painfully aware of the profound difference between my story of call and theirs. I must confess that I was not dragged kicking and screaming into the work of being a preacher. My "call" was something more akin to what happened to the sailors in Homer's *Odyssey* when they heard the sirens' song. I felt lured into the pulpit. From the moment I preached my first sermon, I loved preaching. In fact, as cheesy as it sounds, I think my attraction to preaching started when I was still thinking that I would grow up to be a fireman or a brain surgeon.

I can remember being fascinated by the man in the black robe who got to stand in that elevated wooden box and talk to the congregation. At the beginning of worship, he would mysteriously appear from a hidden door in the wall of the chancel and then take a seat in what looked like a throne. Then, at the end of worship, as the pipe organ triumphantly blared out its song, he would recess down the aisle like a general leading a victory parade. After worship, when my parents would let me, I would walk down to the chancel and sneak into the pulpit. I was too short to see over the top, but hidden behind the walls of that elevated box I would give myself the experience of what it felt like to stand there.

Irrespective of the potentially pathological source of my choice of profession, here I am now twenty-nine years into this life of being a preacher, and I still love it. But I have also at times come to a place of loving to hate it. I love it because I love opening the Scriptures and inviting people to ponder what it means to relate to God. Yet this love is often mitigated by the ever-growing awareness that the pulpit is still one of the best places in the church to hide.

The Pulpit: A Place to Hide

More than anywhere else in the church, the pulpit tempts me to put on my pastoral persona. The work of being up in front of the congregation pulls me in conflicting directions and so inspires in me the temptation to hide. Up there in front of God and the congregation, I am both vulnerable and powerful. There I proclaim the good news, yet I do so through the filter of my own life and experience. There I point to the One who is greater than me, but it is me they are looking at while I am in the process of giving witness. There my job is simply to tell the truth, but as I do so I am ever cognizant of the burden of trying to hold people's attention. So in the wake of preaching, I often feel exhausted, and as I internally debrief the experience, I find myself slipping in and out of the fear that I preached more about me than about the gospel of God.

It would not be overstating the matter to say that after a sermon I sometimes feel a bit like a fraud. Feeling like I have been neither fully true to myself nor fully faithful to the gospel, I shake my head in confusion over the question, Why do I masochistically spend so much energy on the production of this weekly implement of torture? In the face of this tension, the temptation is strong to put on the pastoral persona and hide. If I feel like a fraud, why not just go with that and become one? Put on the costume, play the role, entertain the troops, and dispense those weekly spiritual analgesics that serve only to dull people's pain and encourage them to go back to sleep. Go for the laugh or the tear, but carefully clothe it with an allusion to a biblical text, and people will feel the faintly numinous stirrings of something that approximates the presence of God. Then in the wake of the delivery, listen for that off-screen voice that says, "That's a wrap," descend from the pulpit, call it a day and begin the work of learning the lines for next week's show.

I have a friend in ministry who tells the story of an incredible scene played out at a retirement reception for his predecessor. The man who preceded him as pastor in this congregation had served in the role for more than thirty years. By report of some of the members of this congregation, on the day this man finished his active ministry, he announced to a small gathering of well-wishers: "It's been a great run. But I have to tell you, I haven't really believed a word of it for the last twenty years." And with these inspiring words he moved out of the manse and headed off into his sunset years looking forward, I suppose, to little more than a nirvana of regular rounds of golf and a nightly enjoyment of the cocktail hour.

One could say that he finally came clean, that at least in this last act he took off the persona and chose to be honest. Yet "honesty" came way too late. At this point it was more abusive and vindictive than it was liberating. He may have felt free, but I imagine that most everybody else in the room felt betrayed and duped. Obviously, honesty would have had a more nurturing impact had he admitted this truth to himself and his congregation twenty years earlier. Yet something sustained him in his persona. Donning his false self became the norm. Hiding became more comfortable than an "open statement of the truth" (2 Cor 4:2), and the work of inviting people to wake up to the presence of God atrophied to the point of nonexistence.

Hiding from God

One of the primary themes in the story of our relationship with God is our propensity to hide from God. Once our parents in the Garden felt shame and stopped wanting union with God, they chose to hide. In effect the serpent's invitation was this: "Cover up, run away, let mistrust and fear, rather than gratitude and joy, guide you in your relationship with God." It doesn't take much for the church to become a contemporary version of the fig leaf. It's a great place to hide from God. It can be a very good place to inoculate ourselves with enough religion to keep us insulated from the power and love of God. Pastors hide out in the pulpit and parishioners hide behind their masks of false piety. Close enough to holy things to be anesthetized by religion, we successfully avoid the threat and the reward of an encounter with the living God.

In light of this hazard, as pastors we need enough of the prophet in us to sense and expose this tendency. Above all else, the vocation of the prophet is to be dedicated to the work of calling people to wake up to God. The voice of the prophet issues forth from another Voice, who never stops inviting his people to take up the offer of covenant relationship with himself. Yet this invitation to accept God's offer of life usually has to be prefaced by a word that displaces and blows apart the stunted imaginations of God's people. Good news is preceded by what initially feels like bad news. The precursor to the experience of God's favor is hearing the wake-up call that scatters "the proud in the thoughts of their hearts" (Lk 1:51).

In short, prophets can be annoying to people. The work of confronting sin and inviting people to turn from that sin and toward God is not always greeted with a warm response. Yet for those who have ears to hear it, the bad news of sin can be the beginning of an invitation to listen to the good news of a pathway to life.

Prophetic Preaching

Luke's record of John the Baptist's basic message gives us an illustration of this two-edged sword of the prophetic message. It is a word that, like Jeremiah's word, both tears down and builds up (Jer 1:10). It is both the bad news that rudely awakens God's people from a religiously induced slumber and the good news that invites them to set their lives in the liberating story that dwarfs their miniscule world of religion. It hacks away at what we think is sacred and then shows us where true holiness lies.

There are three paragraphs in Luke's depiction of John's sermon, and in each paragraph I believe we have a description of an important component in prophetic preaching. We have a paradigm that can inform our work as pastors and help us craft sermons that provide true comfort. Part of the message of consolation is confrontation. John's message serves to unmask the idols of religion we create to replace God, expose the hypocrisy in our lives that has been fostered by this lie and invite us to behold how God's story is far greater than anything we could have ever asked for or imagined.

The message begins by unmasking the idol of religion. To say the least, John does not mince words. There is little doubt that he is going for the jugular when he likens his audience to a "brood of vipers" (Lk 3:7) who in their flight from sin are just ahead of the flames of judgment. The image that comes to mind for me is the fires that burn various parts of the foot-hills in Southern California each year. One of my memories of growing up there is watching these fires destroy just about everything in their path.

After the dry summer, the chaparral plants were like fuel waiting for ignition. When that spark came and the Santa Ana winds fanned the flame, this fuel burned hot and fast. As these fires voraciously consumed chamise shrubs and sage brush, the chaparral animals fled before the flames, try-ing to find safety. John is making use of a similar image. In effect, he says, "You are like a bunch of little snakes coming out from under a burning bush. You slither out here to the Jordan to get your fix of forgiveness, but what good is that? You come hoping that this new religion show in the wilder-ness will do the trick. But unless your hearts are changed, what you receive here won't be any better than what you could pay for at the temple."

John was calling people away from a religion of sin man-agement through religious washings and purification rituals. He was inviting them to wholeness and integrity: "Bear fruits worthy of repentance" (Lk 3:8). In other words, "If these rit-uals are signs of a true turning of your heart away from sin and toward God, then let this baptism that I offer come in response to the sign of a changed life. Let this baptism serve to reflect an interior reality. Have you come out to the wil-derness merely in search of the latest version of a religious anesthetic? If so, you might as well head back into town. What I am inviting you to do is much more than merely dull the effect of sin with yet another ritual. Stop running from sin, and turn toward God. Face the One who will transform your lives."

John's deconstruction of religious assumptions continues: "Do not begin to say to yourselves, 'We have Abraham as our ancestor'; for I tell you, God is able from these stones to raise up children to Abraham. Even now the ax is lying at the root of the trees; every tree therefore that does not bear good fruit is cut down and thrown into the fire" (Lk 3:8-9). In other words, do not be lulled into a false sense of security because of your religious pedigree. When it comes to your covenant relationship with God, the facts of history, genealogy and religious practice are not of primary importance. What is important is the condition of our hearts, the congruence between the religious marks we bear and the way we live.

John's sermon was like Jeremiah's call to a circumcision of the heart (Jer 4:4). He had little patience with those who were choosing to remain in a religiously induced slumber and let them know that they were on an unsustainable path: "Even now the ax is lying at the root of the trees" (Lk 3:9). In other words, "Your belief in a stable and rooted place before God will crumble. What you think is unshakable is actually in the process of being felled. So wake up and see that a covenant relationship with your Maker is about more than merely resting in your religious pedigree or availing yourselves of a series of cleansing rituals."

Exposing Religion's "Default" Setting

The prophet's work of shedding light on the reality of sin is most difficult among those who have come to believe they long ago found a way to alleviate the discomfort of this condition. When Jesus is criticized by the religious aristocracy of the day for eating with tax collectors and sinners, he reminds his critics that he has come to heal not those who are well but those who are sick (Mt 9:12). The problem the religious leaders had with hearing him say this was that they could not conceive of themselves as needing what Jesus had to offer. No doubt they would all stipulate that sin was a problem. However, their religious means of managing it had dulled their senses to both the depth of their need and the height of God's grace.

It's amazing how this happens, but the vehicle that is meant to lead us into a transforming covenantal relationship with God can easily become the very thing that makes us deaf to the voice of God. It is easy for us as pastors to think our jobs are primarily about stewarding a religious institution, and it's easy for members of our congregations to believe that church offers a list of spiritual commodities that are theirs by virtue of their status as members. The means to an end becomes an end in itself. Pastors spend their days polishing the religious vessels that adorn the temple and neglect the truth that these vessels are designed to point to something greater than themselves. Parishioners walk into church assuming they will receive the spiritual adrenaline shot they've come to expect. A quick survey of our religious history makes plausible the argument that humanity seems to have a default programming that automatically resets to the place of resting in our religious processes and pedigree rather than actively pursuing relationship with God.

Prophets are called to expose these tendencies. Our preaching needs to awaken people to how narrow and stunted religious perceptions blind us to the "breadth and length and height and depth" of the love of God (Eph 3:18-19). In today's church, this job seems especially relevant. In the fight for survival in our increasingly secular culture, congregations often configure their mission in terms of maintaining or increasing their market share. Our consumer society is good at forming pew sitters who are discerning shoppers.[1] Thus the temptation is strong for us as pastors to settle for providing people with the religion they want rather than the truth they need. Yet prophets have nothing to sell. Our job is not to get people to buy Jesus as if he were some product. Our job is to give witness to the truth. What folks do with that truth is a matter between them and God.

In the face of this pressure to maintain or increase market share, we can take some encouragement from John's story. He clearly had a substantial market share. His popularity is a historical fact. I think there is a reason for this that is not unique to John. Truth may hurt, but it also liberates. When people hear the word of truth that resonates with their souls, they wake up and begin to be on the watch for God. This was certainly true with John's audience. What they were hearing from him was an answer to the most pressing question they had. They wanted to know how to be right with God, and asked, "What then should we do?" (Lk 3:10). If the faithful practice of religious ritual will not make us right with God, then what will? What should our lives look like? Tell us what is missing and how we can obtain it. Help us to understand this emptiness and how God fills it.

John's answer is as straightforward as their question: Don't be hypocrites. Don't claim to be the people of God and then live as if that identity has no relationship with the way you act in the world. Share that extra coat of yours; do your job

---

[1]For an excellent recent treatment of this theme of how our consumer culture influences the attitudes of the American church, see Skye Jethani, *The Divine Commodity* (Grand Rapids: Zondervan, 2009).

with integrity; don't abuse your power. Share with those who have nothing and refuse to take inappropriate advantage of your position (Lk 3:11-14). Since you have been declared righteous, live righteously. Live lives that are congruent with the faith you profess. As people who are in relationship with God, live out all your relationships guided by God's justice and love. John's reply to the people who asked his advice was to give them specific applications of something one of his predecessors once proclaimed: "Do justice, . . . love kindness, and . . . walk humbly with your God" (Mic 6:8).

Although John's theological landscape of Second Temple Judaism was very different from the one we know and proclaim as Christians today, there is in his preaching a note that we would do well to sound. It is the note that helps people understand how relationship with God informs and guides the daily realities of our lives. It is the call to stay awake to the presence of God and see that all of life is lived out in the context of his grace. It is the wake-up call that points out how our practice of religion can lead us to segregate rather than integrate the realms of kingdom and culture. Notice that John did not ask the one with the extra coat to renounce his place of privilege, nor did he call the tax collector to take up another profession, nor did he tell the soldier to end his employment as one of Herod's guards.

Instead he invites each of them to a place of congruence and integrity. He helped them see how their lives fit in the context of God's kingdom. He gave them a window into what it meant to occupy their current place in righteous relationship with God and with others. He gave an example of what it looks like to bear fruit that befits repentance. To do this meant living lives that reflected the change that God was effecting in their hearts. It meant acting in a manner that gave witness to the way relationship with God shapes and organizes our relationships with others in this world.

Reactions to Preaching

Prophetic preaching tells the truth and helps people make spiritual sense of their lives. However, it is hard to abide by this principle in the midst of an era of confusion about what role the sermon should play in today's church. Our fears about declining market share and felt needs lead us to believe that people want practical, "how-to" sermons that cite biblical principles for living. Our Protestant tradition tells us that a sermon is primarily an exposition of a biblical text and that the goal of preaching is to shape a biblically literate and thus (we assume) spiritually mature people. Yet if a sermon is merely the careful exposition of a biblical text with a view to answering theological questions that people may or may not be asking, or if it is merely a bit of advice about how to use biblical principles to navigate the culture successfully, then it will not do much to aid in the formation of disciples. Such sermons may scratch an itch, but they don't invite repentance or faithfulness. They don't land in the deep recesses of a heart that is hungry for God. However, if a sermon gives witness to the truth of God's kingdom and speaks to how living in the awareness of this context can help us relate to God and others as we work with life's everyday questions, it has a better chance of sowing an effective seed.

When preachers do preach a sermon that hits this mark, they can usually expect a reaction. Sometimes people welcome what they have heard and thank the preacher; sometimes they are disturbed by what they have heard and fault the preacher for their discomfort. In either case, the response of the preacher to their reaction ought to be the same, and this leads us to the third paragraph of John's sermon.

People were reacting to John's sermon and it got them thinking and talking about who John might be. As Luke tells us, "People were filled with expectation, and all were questioning in their hearts concerning John, whether he might be the Messiah" (Lk 3:15). The way John responds to this conjecture is instructive. He directs attention away from himself and back onto God: "I baptize you with water; but one who is more powerful than I is coming; I am not worthy to untie the thong of his sandals. He will baptize you with the Holy Spirit and fire" (Lk 3:16). In short, in the face of the temptations associated with the popularity of his ministry, John stays faithful to his calling of "mak[ing] ready a people prepared for the Lord" (Lk 1:17). When attention is directed to him, he redirects that attention to its proper object. He steps out of the way and nods in God's direction so that folks can see whom they are really encountering.

People often respond to our preaching by either treating us like we are the Messiah or blaming us for thinking that we are the Messiah. When the Word hits its mark, people feel it and choose either to embrace it or to start an argument with us in an attempt to avoid it. Yet irrespective of the nature of their response to the Word, we need to greet their reaction with the same message. We need to continue to point to God and give witness to the truth that we have been sent to proclaim. If we take their warm gratitude as if it belongs to us or try to defend ourselves from the wrath they are throwing our way, we are getting in the way of the work they have to do with God. In short, sow the seed and let it be. We have very little if any control over the soil in which a seed lands. Our job is to invite people to wake up to God and then to rest in the expectation that people's engagement with God is the most important fruit of our work.

Where We Point

One of my favorite artistic depictions of John the Baptist is in the crucifixion panel of Matthias Grünewald's Isenheim Altarpiece.[2] The altarpiece was painted in the early 1500s for the chapel of a hospital in Isenheim, Germany, that ministered to the needs of plague victims. In the center it features a depiction of the crucified Jesus that is like nothing I have seen. His wretched, emaciated body is covered with suppurating sores like those from which the plague victims also suffered. His head hangs to one side; his shoulders seem to be dislocated. But it's his hands that especially draw my attention. From his nail-pierced palms his fingers splay out in all directions, pointing to nothing more or less than the excruciating pain that he is suffering. On Jesus' right we see his mother being comforted by the beloved disciple, John, and either Mary Magdalene or Mary of Bethany on her knees, seeming to pray for relief.

On his left we see John the Baptist. John is holding an open book. At John's feet we see an icon of the Lamb of God. His right arm is lifted and with his forefinger he is pointing at the One who is on the cross. John's finger is also what draws my attention in this painting. In the silence of this gesture he calls the viewer to take note of the wretched figure at whom his finger points. "Look here," that pointing

---

[2]For a good discussion of the history and meaning of this artwork, see Henri Nouwen, *Letters to Marc About Jesus* (New York: Harper & Row, 1987), pp. 23-27.

finger seems to say. "Look here and see the One who comes both to join you in your suffering and to die in order to take it away. Behold the Lamb of God who takes away the sins of the world."

John's bony finger in Grünewald's painting is an image of the essence of our prophetic work. We point at Truth. We direct people's attention to God. As we do so we remind them of the tandem truths of their brokenness and God's grace. These things come together in the cross of Jesus and, as the apostle Paul says, when we as pastor-prophet decide "to know nothing among [our congregations] except Jesus Christ, and him crucified" (1 Cor 2:2), we faithfully do the work of helping people wake up to God. Our job is to give witness and get out of the way. Like John we say, "Don't look at me; look to my right. Look at Jesus."

People may or may not want to stare into the face of the crucified Christ. By confronting people with an invitation to contemplate the ugliness of the cross, we may be providing a catalyst that justifies their decision to turn away. Yet in averting their eyes from the cross, they will also become blind to both their own sin and the healing power of God's love. The cross of Jesus is at once a repulsive and compelling image. It both reflects back to us a picture of our brokenness and sin, and gives witness to God's relentless invitation to us to receive the gift of his steadfast love. It confronts us with an ugly truth and consoles us with a divine assurance. It is both profoundly bad news and liberating good news, and prophets need to be in the business of declaring both.

Luke's editorial coda on John's sermon always brings a smile to my face. After a sermon filled with the harsh images of an unquenchable fire burning off useless chaff and an ax hacking away at the roots of a tree, Luke concludes with the words: "So, with many other exhortations, [John] proclaimed the good news to the people" (Lk 3:18). These are not images that I would normally associate with the idea of good news or consolation. They do not initially invite me to a place of peace. Yet they do wake me up, and once awake I am ready to hear the word that penetrates the wilderness of my life. I am ready to acknowledge this God who is in the business of redemption and transformation. God has made and is making his way to us. This is true consolation. What a privilege, what a joy, what a sobering responsibility it is to be one who is called by God to give witness to it.

7

CONFLICT

Trusting Truth Versus Fearing Instability

And Herodias had a grudge against [John], and wanted to kill him.
But she could not, for Herod feared John, knowing that he was a righteous and
holy man, and he protected him. When he heard him, he was greatly perplexed;
and yet he liked to listen to him. But an opportunity came when Herod on his
birthday gave a banquet for his courtiers and officers and for the leaders of
Galilee. When his daughter Herodias came in and danced, she pleased
Herod and his guests; and the king said to the girl, "Ask me for
whatever you wish, and I will give it." And he solemnly swore
to her, "Whatever you ask me, I will give you, even half
of my kingdom." She went out and said to her mother,
"What should I ask for?" She replied,
"The head of John the baptizer."

MARK 6:19-24

In a world where sound bites and spin are the common cur-
rency of public discourse, the prophetic message is a rare
commodity. Our politicians have learned well the lesson that
only a portion of what they say makes its way onto the wire
services, broadcasts and blogs; thus, in as few words as pos-

sible, they attempt to deliver what sounds like the most co-
gent and yet least controversial message. Of course, it is fear
that drives this whole process: fear that if one says too much
or is too clear about a position on a given issue, then one
becomes a target. So to avoid this status, the best strategy
seems to be to touch down briefly but never land. In an attempt to stave off the potential unpleasantness of conflict,
little is said that could actually foster disagreement.

In this environment, pastors need to learn the valuable
lesson of not taking their communication cues from the
world. Whereas sound bites and spin are designed to avoid
conflict, prophetic sermons almost always engender it. The
fear of instability that dominates choices around what is said
in public discourse has no place in the world of the prophet.
Conflict is the inevitable outcome of good ministry, because
if the gospel is being preached, things are probably going to
get shaken up. The irony of the good news of the coming of
God's kingdom is that it causes an earthquake.

Offering the Bad News That's Good News

The comforting cry that breaks into the silence of the wilderness in Isaiah 40 is a word that changes the face of the landscape. To preach the kingdom is to call people's attention to
the truth that their lives are set in a context that is greater
than the one they have created for themselves. This is a message that reorders life. Thus the "comfort" we are to announce
is initially rather uncomfortable.

When Jeremiah is called by God to bring God's message to
Judah, he is told that he will be involved in a work that will
both "pluck up" and "plant" (Jer 1:10). Such is the work of a
prophet. There is a message of deconstruction that precedes

the news of reconstruction. There is in prophetic proclamation both the initial bad news of a world gone awry and the hope-filled good news of God setting things right. Both aspects of this message are invitations to wake up—first to the destabilizing truth that we are not at the center of our world and second to the liberating truth that it is God who occupies this space.

Therefore, if the avoidance of controversy and the maintenance of the appearance of stability is our aim, it's a safe bet that we will not venture very far into the work of being a prophet. Instead we will find ourselves in spaces of anxiety about abstractions such as the well-being of "the ministry" or "the good of the congregation," but the real work of connecting people with the earth-shattering good news of God's invitation to an eternal covenant relationship will have little space in our schedule. Our calling is to trust the truth of our message rather than to fear the unpleasantness that comes when people initially deal with waking up.

Over the past seven years, my family and I have had the experience of being volunteer puppy raisers for Guide Dogs for the Blind. We have had five female Labrador puppies in our home who joined us when they were eight weeks old and left us when they were about fourteen or fifteen months old. Our job with these dogs was to socialize them, teach them some basic commands and bond with them.

These puppies have taught us a great deal about life. One of the more profound lessons has come as a result of helping a puppy grow into the awareness that she is not the center of the world. It is a gentle process of asserting dominance and becoming the puppy's "pack leader." We do this in a variety of ways, but irrespective of which exercise we use, the goal is the same: establish the puppy in the initially disturbing but ultimately liberating truth that she belongs to a reality that is bigger than herself. Initially, when the puppy doesn't know these boundaries, things can be a bit chaotic. When she doesn't yet know that we are going to care for her and protect her and establish a place for her, she is a bit wild. She also initially resists living within the boundaries.

One of the other volunteers related a story about how she chose to work with an especially dominant male in her charge. On a few occasions (because it only took a few occasions) while the puppy slept, she gently pushed him out of the place where he was lying and sat down in that spot herself. When the puppy awakened enough to figure out what was going on, he had to deal with the truth that this place he occupied was not just his place. This particular raiser said that the look on the puppy's face was priceless. Ears perked up, eyes focused on her, tail up but not wagging, almost as if he was pondering how to respond. His definition of his territory had been challenged, and the choice was now between attempting to reclaim it and sharing it. No doubt the fact that the hand that fed him was the one pushing him off the pillow was the reason he opted for the latter.

When people are pushed to consider the truth that their lives are set in a context bigger than the one they define or control, they tend to push back. It initially feels threatening to have to make space for this truth. Yet if people can get beyond the initial threat, they can experience the truth of how the boundary lines of the kingdom of God actually fall in "pleasant places" (Ps 16:6). It is the work of the prophet to proclaim this initially uncomfortable comfort, and this work can lead us into conflict. The hearers of this message often confuse the message and the messenger, and react to us rather than to the God who is issuing the message. Thus, like Jeremiah, we may occasionally find ourselves in some contemporary version of that empty but muddy cistern, waist deep in the sludge of a parishioner's animosity (Jer 38:6). Or, like John, we may find ourselves subject to the earthly powers of one who is engaged in the futile attempt to sustain the lie that he is the center of the world.

Why John Lost His Head

The story of John the Baptist's death is one of the great tragedies of the New Testament. His final encounter with Herod is a rich tale of narcissistic fear engaged in a ridiculous attempt to deny and overthrow an unassailable truth. Mark does a good job of telling this story in very few words. In fact, its brevity intensifies the picture of the pathetic banality of Herod's supposed power. Here is a man who was desperate to preserve the illusion that he was in charge. Yet it is clear that he was totally controlled by the whims of his wicked wife and the fear of looking weak. For Herod the message that he was not the center of his world felt like bad news and, in an attempt to protect himself from the destabilizing effect of this message, he chose to kill the messenger.

Like the stories of Jesus before Pilate and Paul before Agrippa (Jn 18–19; Acts 25–26), the story of John's encounter with Herod is a picture of God's truth exposing and seeping into the cracks in the façade of earthly power. While Herod was supposedly in charge, this story reveals the truth that a competition between two greater powers actually held sway over his decisions. As he was pulled between his respect for John and the desires of his wife, Herod's power was ultimately rendered impotent.

I remember a time when I read Mark 6 out loud in a class where I was teaching on the text. As I read, it was almost as if I could hear people's attention to the text deepen. The room seemed to become increasingly silent. By the time I had finished reading, it felt like a cloud of pathos was hanging over us. My guess is that we were all experiencing anger and grief over the injustice of it all and at the same time embarrassed by the wicked and yet banal weakness of Herod's act.

The scenes in this drama march toward a horrific yet inevitable conclusion: Herod's drooling response to his stepdaughter's dance, Herodias's surreptitious meeting with her daughter to secure what she wants, and finally Herod's pitiful attempt to mask his weakness with a desperate show of strength in granting the girl's request for John's head. Narcissism seems to be the great winner that day. Fearful of losing face in the presence of his guests, Herod yields to his stepdaughter's demand. In the scene that follows, the frivolity in the room was no doubt silenced when the bleeding head of John the Baptist was paraded before them on a platter.

Prophets have one job: to give witness to the truth and entrust the hearers of the message to God. Obviously, pointing to truth can be a risky business, and the rub of the risk is in the wild card of people's response. The sleeping dog doesn't have to come to the conclusion that he is not at the center of his world and thus needs to share his space. He can lash out. Fear of this sort of response is what often tempts us to manage conflict in one of two ways: either we seek a path that avoids it in the first place or we hit back just as hard in order to protect or justify ourselves.

Both of these responses betray our lack of trust in the redemptive and loving power of God. For both demonstrate that we are not primarily concerned with people's response to the gospel, but with people's response to us as pastors. When either keeping my job or fulfilling my vision for my church becomes my primary motivator, I have stopped participating in the work of God. I have stopped depending on God to work through me.

Why We Avoid the Truth

There are times in the life of a pastor when it seems much easier to avoid telling the truth. Of course, by kingdom standards, this choice is always foolish. Truth frees us, after all (Jn 8:31-32). Yet the burden of truth is sometimes hard to bear, and the anticipation of this heaviness often leads us to that place where we want to avoid stating the obvious.

In more than one congregation I have served, I have had to speak with people who were violating their marriage vows and choosing to have extramarital affairs. In all of these situations I dealt with the temptation to sweep the matter under the rug. Why confront it? The affair was only the final manifestation of a relationship that had gone bad years before. Stuff happens, so let's just move on. Why address it? Why engage the parties involved in it? What's done is done; we might as well bring down the curtain on it all and get on with the business of living. After all, we're about grace here, and we all know that grace covers a multitude of sin.

The temptation to fear. There are all sorts of reasons I am tempted to take such a path, but they all find their way back to the primary motivation of fear. I am afraid of what will happen when the hidden mess becomes a visible mess. I am afraid of strained relationships and of being disliked. I am afraid of getting in the middle of something that is not mine to manage. I am afraid of the destabilizing effect such information will have on the congregation. In short, I am afraid because I see myself, and not God, as the one who has to make this all better. While I know that the situation was created apart from me, and in many ways has nothing to do with me, as pastor I experience this odd temptation to become the redeemer of it all. And since I know intuitively that I can't be the redeemer, I conclude that the best course is to turn my back and say nothing. I avoid the conflict because I know I don't have the power to resolve it.

I remember a time in one congregation when, following the revelation of a high-profile extramarital affair, I went to two elders to obtain some advice on how to handle the matter. Anger and fear were my companions when I walked into that meeting. I approached these two elders because I needed them to know and because I needed their advice as to how to respond. I was furious with the couple, and I was fearful about the effect their choice would have on the life and health of the congregation. I was convinced that a disaster had taken place that would lead to the dismantling of all the gains we had made, and I needed these two elders to help me manage the crisis and maintain our congregational equilibrium.

When I walked into that meeting, they no doubt saw the concern on my face, and at first they each mirrored that concern with an equal level of seriousness. Yet as I let the story unfold, I watched what I deemed to be a strange, if not inappropriate, lifting of their countenance. As I finished the story and posed the question, "So, what should I do?" one of them responded. "You know, David, it's just sin." At first it seemed like a positively ridiculous, not to mention condescending, rejoinder to my revelation. Why was he minimizing the gravity of this situation and belittling me in the process? Of course it's sin. But *just* sin? What did he mean by that? I initially received the comment as if it were a pat on my head wedded with an admonition not to worry. I heard him telling me to grow up, and at that moment I thought I had made a great error in choosing to seek the counsel of these elders. To be honest, I initially wondered if the nonchalance of this remark was signaling the presence of a similar kind of secret in the life of this elder.

Yet the more I sat with the remark, the more its wisdom became clear. The subtext under this statement was a question: What are you afraid of? It's just sin. In other words, why are you taking on what you have no power to take on, and why aren't you trusting God to handle what he is in the business of handling? Don't try to fix this or manage this or clean up this mess; just name it and let God take care of it, because he can do that a lot better than you.

What initially seemed like condescension and indifference suddenly became a loving admonition to trust the truth that I was in the business of proclaiming. I hasten to point out that trusting this truth and being willing to act in light of it did not make my life as pastor of this congregation easier. Initially it meant that things got a lot messier. It meant having to live in the mess that is produced by our sin. It meant speaking to people who did not want me speaking to them, as well as engaging other congregants who were talking about and taking up sides in the matter. It meant conflict, because we all dealt with yet another example of how none of us is the center of our own world.

We had to make space for the testing of our faith in the God who occupies this center. We had to learn once again that there is One who is bigger than—and therefore who can handle—our sin. Trusting this One reduced the threat of the conflict to its proper proportions. Once I was dispossessed of the job of managing it, I was free to live with the mess and trust the God who was with us and still at work among us even in the midst of it.

The temptation to become a warrior. A second temptation in the face of conflict is to become a warrior. When we become warriors we settle into a strategy of engaging conflict with the objective of winning the adoption of our way, often to the neglect of trusting in God's way.

As pastors we live in a realm where the stakes always seem high. We are, after all, giving witness to the truth of the living God. Therefore, when people are ignoring or living in opposition to this truth, we naturally feel the need to try to convince them to change their minds. There is nothing wrong with vigorously engaging in debate, yet it is easy for debate to cross the line into the realm of a battle where the stakes are no longer about God's truth but about the personalities of those who are fighting for their interpretation of it.

When a conflict situation becomes the struggle to win by getting people to see it my way, I as a pastor have displaced God and taken up residence in a place where I do not belong. Instead of proclaiming the truth and entrusting people to God, I am assuming the authority over the work of securing their decision for God. In so doing, I have stopped deferring to the One who occupies the center and instead have put myself in that place, for it is their response to me that is now at issue, and God is somewhere on the periphery.

Making the move from the edges, where we do the prophetic work of pointing to the Center, to the place of occupying the center ourselves is a relatively easy journey. It's not hard for the simplest and most insignificant of battles in the church to usher us into this place. When we as pastors have thought through the theology behind what we want to do in ministry and have come to the conclusion that a particular program or ministry is the right way to accomplish God's purposes in the world, we tend to be a bit dogmatic and rigid about our conclusions. We may have good reason to dwell in this place of certainty about our conclusions. We might be able to frame a perfect biblical justification for our choices. We might, in short, be "right." Yet when proving ourselves right becomes the primary objective of our conflict, we have crossed the line into narcissism and demonstrated our lack of trust in the ultimate victory of God.

Good intentions and good theology notwithstanding, when I enter the battle merely for the sake of winning, it usually becomes about me and not the issue itself. It doesn't matter if I am right. Arguing harder and better doesn't help. What's more, if I am the "winner" in such conflicts, the net gain usually shows in the minus rather than the plus column. Winning in this way usually means damage to, if not the destruction of, my pastoral relationship with the person over whom I have been victorious. In short, it does no good to win the battle and lose the war.

Paul Handles Conflict

Paul's experience with the Corinthian church has been one of the most valuable pointers to me in situations when I am facing the temptation to deal with conflict by donning the mantle of a warrior. In his second letter to this congregation especially, I have found both guidance to avoid the temptation and comfort in knowing that Paul struggled with it as well. What I love most about this letter is that Paul gives some of the best advice a pastor could get about how to trust God in the face of conflict with a congregation, yet his struggle to follow his own advice is palpable.

Clearly Paul is frustrated with the people of Corinth, and in the midst of that frustration we see him moving back and forth on the continuum stretched between the two points of trusting God and needing the Corinthians to affirm the rightness of his ministry. On the one hand, he humbly acknowledges that any competence he has comes from God and on the other hand, in what seems to be a moment of weakness, he lets them know about the superiority of his own spiritual experience in comparison to their own (2 Cor 3:4-5; 12:1-4). While he steadfastly maintains that he is not trying to "commend" himself to them, he is clearly trying to convince them of the rightness of his particular path. At times he seems comfortable with stating the truth and entrusting them to God, and at times he almost seems to grab them verbally by the shoulders and demand that they listen to him.

Even though Paul's frustration with Corinth is palpable, it does not send him running from the room, shaking his head, tearing his garments and crying out, *"Icabod!"* ("The glory of the Lord has departed!"). Instead he stays engaged as he releases the Corinthian church into God's hands and says,

> But thanks be to God, who in Christ always leads us in
> triumphal procession, and through us spreads in every

place the fragrance that comes from knowing him. For we are the aroma of Christ to God among those who are being saved and among those who are perishing; to the one a fragrance from death to death, to the other a fragrance from life to life. Who is sufficient for these things? For we are not peddlers of God's word like so many; but in Christ we speak as persons of sincerity, as persons sent from God and standing in his presence. (2 Cor 2:14-17)

In other words, our ministry is never about winning. It's about understanding ourselves to be the defeated slaves of Jesus being paraded like prizes of war through the streets of the victorious army upon their return from battle. Jesus Christ is the triumphant general, and we are in his tow. As his followers, we give off his scent. We smell like Jesus, and that scent may or may not be received as a pleasant aroma.

At play here is the same gentle but unavoidable gesture that we see illustrated in the tilted head and gesturing hands of the icon of St. John the Forerunner. Paul changes the metaphor from the sense of sight to the sense of smell, but he is saying the same thing: There's Jesus; deal with him. Direct your attention to him because he's the one with whom you have business to conduct, not us. We'll do our best to tell the truth as we know it. But we're not in this to win some prize, or to get our way, or to be proven right, or to chalk up another sale. We're in this because we know that he is the Truth. So take in a deep breath and let us know what you smell. It is up to you to determine whether or not you like the smell and wish to deal with him.

Over and over in this letter, Paul directs our steps in the

matter of handling conflict with our congregations. In chapter 6 of the letter, he makes an appeal: "Our heart is wide open to you. . . . Open wide your hearts also" (2 Cor 6:11, 13). The very best thing we can do as pastors is declare the truth as we know it and remain open to relationship with the ones to whom we are preaching, whether they take up what we have to say or not.

As Paul faced accusations from Corinth that he was arrogant, as he listened to their criticisms of his personal appearance and as he was subjected to their suspicions that his spirituality came from a lower plane than theirs, his best response was to be vulnerable and to ask them to respond in kind. Open wide your hearts also; engage with us and trust Jesus. In essence he decided that his encounter with them was not going to be about winning but about being led by the One who has won the greatest victory.

Facing Injustice

Easily said, but let's face it, it's hard to let Jesus be the winner, or even the loser for that matter, especially when it feels like we are the ones fighting the battle and not him. A parishioner's animosity directed at me in the wake of hearing a word from God that he would have preferred not to hear is not a very rewarding gift. The hardest thing to endure in the midst of conflicts with members of our congregation is that as pastors we often feel misunderstood or misrepresented, and no amount of reasonable discourse seems to have any impact on changing these perceptions. There is a certain injustice to it all. And if this is all faithfulness gets me, I find myself wondering how long I can sustain this gig. Why do we have to endure the wrath that is really intended for the

One who is the source of the message? Clearly, we are not on a level playing field, and that feels unfair.

However, before we pastors start feeling too sorry for ourselves about this imbalance, we need to recognize that neither do we lose our heads nor are we cast into a pit as a result of this unfairness. As the writer of Hebrews reminds us, "In your struggle against sin you have not yet resisted to the point of shedding your blood" (Heb 12:4). The great cloud of witnesses who have gone before us and are now cheering us on have in most cases engaged in a fiercer battle than we have (Heb 12:1-2). Yet the point of this is not a guilt-inducing comparison; the point is to run with endurance the same race that they ran. It is to fix our eyes on the One who is the winner and to understand that even our apparent loss can be the first step toward a kind of winning that is not of this world.

There is nothing in Mark 6 that gives us any indication about how John dealt with the injustice he was suffering. We have no record of psalms of complaint that he may have written while in jail. His disciples did not record and preserve any jeremiads he may have preached against the injustices he suffered. We do have the question of clarification that John directs to Jesus from jail in Luke 7 (to which we will turn our attention in the next chapter). Yet here in Mark 6, all we have from John is silence.

In its own way, this silence proclaims a truth that we pastors need to take into account. To put it bluntly, the matter of what John may have thought about how he was being treated was really not the point. For this is not a story about John. It is a story about the darkness of the world into which the light of God shines. It is an illustration of how the prophet stands between two truths and gives witness to both. The prophet must point to the truth of both the depth of human wickedness and sin on one side and the power of God's inextinguishable light on the other. John's thoughts and reflections about the injustice he was suffering would add nothing to the proclamation of these truths. His work was never about winning a following or establishing an ongoing movement. It was the work of giving witness to truth: making ready a people who were waking up to and thus preparing for an encounter with the living God.

The potential tragedy of prophetic pastoral ministry is born of the same source that gives birth to what we might call our victory. For all the conflict that the work of giving witness might create, it is also the source of liberty for us as ministers. If the task before us is primarily to point to the truth of God, we have nothing to lose if we give ourselves faithfully to this work. Whether people pay attention or not, whether they react to the Word with approbation or contempt really doesn't matter. What matters from our end is the work of giving witness to the light. What matters is the elucidation of both the despair behind us and the hope on the horizon toward which we journey. Whether we accompany folks for the entirety of this journey is really not the point of our work. The prophet, like Moses or Martin Luther King Jr., has to be willing to see and declare the view from the mountaintop without necessarily being able to get to the other side.

8

CONFUSION

Risking Doubt Versus Denying Dissonance

The disciples of John reported all these things to him. So John summoned two of his disciples and sent them to the Lord to ask, "Are you the one who is to come, or are we to wait for another?" When the men had come to him, they said, "John the Baptist has sent us to you to ask, 'Are you the one who is to come, or are we to wait for another?'" Jesus had just then cured many people of diseases, plagues, and evil spirits, and had given sight to many who were blind. And he answered them, "Go and tell John what you have seen and heard: the blind receive their sight, the lame walk, the lepers are cleansed, the deaf hear, the dead are raised, the poor have good news brought to them. And blessed is anyone who takes no offense at me."

LUKE 7:18-23

Conflict with those who have been unsettled by hearing God's truth is not the only form of conflict that the prophet engages. Sometimes the conflict that rages within us is a much more formidable foe. For any number of reasons, there will be times when we are led to question God's call. In these moments, the Voice that once seemed so clear becomes more like an enigmatic whisper inviting us to reconsider the very things to which we have dedicated our lives. Confidence for ministry borne of hearing a single voice is shaken by an initially confusing conversation of voices. The effect of these competing voices is a dissonance that diminishes the clarity of God's call and makes us begin to wonder if we failed to hear it correctly in the first place.

Voices That Question Our Call

It is especially difficult to engage these competing voices when they come from a reliable and respected source. Such was the case for me when, during our time at Michillinda, my wife, Mary Ann, began to approach me with an observation about a conflict between my calling as a preacher and my role as a husband and father. She shared a perception that was initially very difficult for me to take in. I pushed it away at first, because it felt like taking it in was going to displace a central piece of who I knew myself to be.

Though this thing to which she was giving witness was initially hard to hear, it ultimately proved to be liberating. She opened my eyes to something that I had failed to see and, while in the process of examining it, I wondered if what I had sensed to be God's call was actually nothing more than the sound of my own voice.

Over a period of time, it had become harder and harder for Mary Ann to come to worship and listen to my sermons. What she began to share with me was that my preaching left her feeling unsettled and even a bit angry. As she continued to unpack these feelings with me, she told me that listening to my sermons made her feel exposed and vulnerable. It was as if I was using our life together as a family primarily as the context in which to generate my sermons. The subtext of each sermon seemed to her to be something that we'd been experiencing the prior week, and it seemed like I was broadcasting our family's life to the congregation.

She also observed that the actual process of me writing my sermon each week was becoming intolerably intense. To her, I felt absent. Although I was physically present, it was as if I was mainly around as an observer who was looking for material for Sunday. All of this added up to one big question for her, and she began to ask it: "How are we going to go forward as a family if this is happening every week?" Her obvious but unstated rejoinder was, "I'm pretty sure I can't."

My initial reaction to this revelation was argumentative denial. After all, I wasn't telling lots of stories about my family and exposing the details of our lives in my sermons. In terms of actual content, I was careful not to violate any of those rules about good boundaries. I concluded that Mary Ann was just being overly sensitive. Obviously no one in the congregation was picking up what she feared they might be picking up. They couldn't possibly hear the subtext that she heard and make those connections without having been present in our home that week. What's more, how could I not allow our lives of the last week to have an impact on the content of my sermon? Integrity in preaching seemed to demand that kind of interaction.

Finally, my response to the accusation about intensity was, Well, that's just the way it is. Preaching is intense, and I'm not sure I can do anything about lessening that intensity without also diminishing the value of the finished product. In short, my initial gut response was, "You knew who and what I was when you married me, so what's changed and why can't you deal with that now?" A voice was questioning what I had assumed to be the unquestionable Voice, and all I wanted to do was deny the source of the dissonance.

Well, as any good marriage therapist will tell you, to persist in this course would not have yielded good fruit. And we had had enough good marriage therapy for me to come to this conclusion without making the mistake of digging my trench of denial too deep. By the grace of God and love from and for Mary Ann, I decided that I needed to listen to this threatening voice.

It will come as no surprise to anyone that I discovered that this voice had something to teach me. I resisted it at first because I was afraid. I feared that making space for Mary Ann's observation was going to force a choice between being a pastor and remaining married to her. I didn't want to give up either. Yet what I began to apprehend was that this voice was actually calling me more deeply into both my work as a pastor and my identity as a husband. It took the mask off one of my idols, namely preaching, and helped me see that God's call in my life was to something much bigger and more enduring than simply being a preacher.

Questioning Is Imperative

There is much more of this story that could be told. For now it is enough to make the point that as pastors we will not live into God's call without that call being questioned. We cannot embark on the journey of answering God's invitation to give witness to his kingdom without encountering obstacles. Those apparent barriers sometimes plant the suggestion that just maybe we didn't hear quite right. They sow a seed of doubt about our calling, and we wonder if God's call to us has changed or if we failed to hear it correctly in the first place. Yet the thing to do with this potentially confusing mix of messages is not to deny the dissonance but to make space for the competing voice.

Jeremiah provides us with a very good example of making space for this dissonance. Following a beating and a night in the stocks at the hands of the high priest, Pashhur, Jeremiah complains to God. In Jeremiah 20:7-18, we are allowed to view Jeremiah's inner turmoil. With the rapidity of a ping-pong ball being beaten back and forth over the net, we see Jeremiah bounce off the two competing forces that seem to govern his life. The voices of Pashhur and other detractors are calling him to shut up and hang it up, while the word of God compels him to preach.

It is all poignantly summed up in verse 9: "If I say, 'I will not mention him, or speak any more in his name,' then within me there is something like a burning fire shut up in my bones; I am weary with holding it in, and I cannot." Jeremiah bounces between cursing God for what feels like a betrayal and praising God for the gift of deliverance. He moves from accusing God of seducing him to praising God as his dread warrior and protector. He sings a song of thanksgiving to his Creator and a song of lament that curses the day he was born. Without explanation or resolution, these competing voices are held together throughout the text, and as readers we are made painfully aware of the obvious truth that Jeremiah was one conflicted dude.

Yet in the unresolved tension of these polarities we find the encouragement to persevere in our call as prophets. The un-apologetic and unexplained coexistence of these two compet-ing voices in one man serves to vindicate a common experience among pastors. The circumstances that arise out of acting on our calling inevitably lead us to question that calling, and in the struggle of this conflict we learn something more about God and about ourselves that fosters our own spiritual growth. In short, in these times of inner conflict, we would do well to recognize that God is doing something in us that will ultimately enrich all that God will do through us.

The stakes are high in these periods of dissonance. At issue is not just the content of what we think God is calling us to do. What is at stake is who we perceive God to be. It isn't just our identity that is in question in these moments. We wonder not just if we heard God right. We wonder if we want to continue listening at all. For, like Jeremiah, in those moments we are not clear whether God is our seducer or deliverer. What's more, we're not even sure we want to take the risk of finding out one way or the other. Things have so radically changed, expectations have been so radically altered, identities have been so radically called into question, we are not sure what our next step should be.

Responses to Doubts About Calling

Denial. In the face of this doubt, we have some choices about how to respond. One of the choices we can make is to deny its presence and try to muscle through it. We argue that faith in God's call to us demands that we push aside these nagging doubts and competing voices because they deny what we know is right and true. So we don the warrior's garb and go to battle with this nasty voice that is tempting us away from ministry. Kidding ourselves into the belief that we can ignore this voice, we put on the façade of strength and continue our work.

The garb of the warrior is really nothing more than our "pastoral persona," and when we trust only in this mask, we cease to do effective work. As James Loder used to say, "The secret always secretes."[1] What we try to push away or deny always seeps out somewhere else, and any futile attempt to try to plug up these cracks in our armor diverts our attention from doing the very work we are trying to protect. To make this choice is to live with a divided heart, and this is the beginning of the end of effective service as a pastor.

Running away. Another choice we can make is to fixate on the dilemma and run from God's call. When we make this choice, we seek to resolve the dilemma by removing the source of the conflict. We react primarily to the fear that we are not and never have been called, and we get out as fast as we can.

As with the first choice, to make this choice is to see oneself both at the center of the problem and as the primary effecter of a solution. If the first choice is relying only on our power to resolve the tension, the second choice is focusing only on our weakness and concluding there is no reason to fight. Feeling like fools for ever having believed we actually heard God's voice, we run from God and the church. We retreat into a perceived safe place where the dissonance is silenced because our history is denied. Again the result is a divided heart as we live with the nagging "what ifs" of an unfinished story.

Going to God. Obviously the best choice we can make is to engage the dissonance and go right to God with the ques-

---

[1]James Loder was a professor at Princeton Theological Seminary, and I heard him offer this observation in a class he was teaching called "The Holy Spirit and Human Transformation."

tions that emerge from it. The sound of a competing voice is obviously no threat to God. This One who laughs at the feeble machinations of the kings of the earth (Ps 2) can certainly handle the questions we bring. So, what we must do is seek clarity from the One who called us. As in any good relationship, we have to check things out with the other. We must assume the same posture as the prophet Habakkuk and move to the watchtower and wait to see how God might answer (Hab 2:1). Both Jeremiah and John the Baptist join with Habakkuk and make this third choice.

Discovering Who God Is Not
In his prison cell in Herod's house, John no doubt had plenty of time to reflect, and Luke tells us that this reflection gave rise to a question. In the depressive darkness of a jail cell, it is not hard to imagine that John's thoughts went to failure. "Did I get this right or not? This one whom I have proclaimed to be the Deliverer isn't doing much to show himself as such. Why isn't he in Jerusalem? What's he doing milling about in Galilee with lepers and tax collectors and fishermen? I've staked my life on believing I am supposed to be about the work of pointing to him, but now I wonder if maybe I'm directing people's gaze in the wrong direction."

Of course, this inner dialogue is all speculation. We do not really know precisely what John expected of Jesus. New Testament scholars debate the specifics of what John meant in his apocalyptic preaching and who and what he thought the Messiah would be and do. Yet, based on Luke's report, what we can conclude is that something was present in Jesus that did not jive with John's expectations concerning the identity and ministry of the Messiah.

So John sends some of his disciples to Jesus with that question: "Are you the one who is to come, or are we to wait for another?" It is a question loaded with many other questions: "Did I hear God's call accurately? Did I discern God's work correctly? Did I invite people to pay attention to the right thing? Here, at what appears to be the end of my life, do I have something to celebrate and rest in or just something to lament and regret?"

When we are ushered into the space where we are given cause to suspect that God may not have spoken to us in the way we have previously perceived and thus may be different from who we have expected him to be, we find ourselves confronted with the challenge of not just how but to whom we are going to pray. Unfulfilled expectations and failed plans in ministry put us in touch with feelings like those expressed by the two disciples heading out of Jerusalem on the road to Emmaus after Jesus' crucifixion. With a sigh of sadness they exhale the words "We had hoped . . ." (Lk 24:21), and in the face of this disappointment, the best plan of action seems to be to get out of town as quickly as possible in the hope of leaving behind the pain.

Luke's telling of this story seems to suggest that the death of Jesus on a Roman cross violated every expectation about the Messiah that these disciples had carried. He was not at all who they thought he would be. So is it any wonder that when he shows up, they don't recognize him? Blinded by their projections of who Jesus should have been, they are initially unable to apprehend the reality of who he in fact is. But disappointment was in this case the precursor of discovery. Articulating and then letting go of those projections was a first step in the process of seeing the Jesus who really was and is.

Based on both my experience and pastoral observation of others, it has occurred to me more than once that people are often invited to a deeper journey of spiritual growth by their discoveries of who God is not. The disorientation that comes from the dissonance is an uncomfortable but familiar step in the process of spiritual formation. When we are confronted with the truth that God is not at all like what we might have expected him to be, when we have to face a crisis where God has not come through for us in the ways that we had hoped and believed he would, we are invited to let go of our projections and make space in our lives for the God who truly is. I see John's experience as being illustrative of this dynamic, and as we pay attention to him, we learn something about how to engage the familiar but unwelcome companion of doubt.

Our First Tool: Prayer

The best thing to do with doubt is to express it, to follow John's lead and check things out with Jesus. When we are struggling with questions about who God is, or how God works, or what God has called us to do, the best thing to do is to go to the only One who can answer these questions and ask. John takes the risk of expressing his doubt to Jesus and in so doing teaches us about how this experience of dissonance is, above all else, an invitation to prayer. Prayer is our first tool in the work of engaging doubt.

Relating directly to the God about whom and for whom we have questions is the fuel we need to sustain the prophetic work of giving witness. We must never forget that our ministry is as much about what God is doing in us as it is about what God is doing through us. Our work is to give witness to the grace in which we stand. A characterization of pastoral ministry that grows out of a perception of God as a distant king who gives us our marching orders and then expects not to have to be engaged again, a God who cares not so much for us but mainly about how we can be deployed for his mission, is a sure recipe for burnout and despair. Yet if we see ourselves as followers of Jesus who are on the lookout for and ready to participate in the ever-expanding work that he is doing, we find ourselves energized as we play our unique part in a miracle that is far more than we could have asked for or expected.

The repetitive nature of our tasks as pastors tempts us into the place of perceiving our work to be very knowable and routine. Shaped by the rhythms of the year and the passages of life, our work can seem a bit static. Another Christmas, another Easter; another baptism, another death; another sermon, another Bible study; another appointment, another meeting. It doesn't take long before we find ourselves in the same place as the preacher in Ecclesiastes: "What has been is what will be, and what has been done is what will be done; there is nothing new under the sun" (Eccles 1:9).

Our Second Tool: Seeing the Kingdom's Dynamism

Yet while the work itself may seem repetitive, we need to keep in mind that there is nothing static about the work that is being done by the Spirit of God in and through this context. Where the Spirit of God is active, we can expect a dynamism and levels of innovation and creativity that are beyond our wildest imagination. We need to live in the flexible space of understanding that ministry—and our call—do not always look the same. God is always in the business of demonstrating to us how his kingdom is bigger than we think.

To remind myself of this truth, I recall a metaphor that encourages me to hold loosely to what I think I see and to remain open to what I may not yet have apprehended. The image I think of is the big, red, neon "Jesus Saves" sign that used to sit atop the Church of the Open Door in downtown Los Angeles. The Church of the Open Door and the Biblical Institute of Los Angeles (BIOLA) were like ground zero for fundamentalism in Southern California in the early to mid-twentieth century. The voices of preachers like Louis Talbot and J. Vernon McGee emanated from its auditorium and went out over the airwaves. The building itself was a beacon of the message proclaimed inside.

As time went on, high rises began to dwarf the building, but its "Jesus Saves" sign continued to burn with the proclamation of its core confession. The building and its sign were still in place in the early 1980s when I was a student at Fuller Seminary. On occasion, especially in celebration of the end of finals, a group of us would head downtown to the Bonaventure Hotel to celebrate. The Bonaventure had one of those revolving lounges on top, and as we sat there together taking in the panorama of LA, that sign atop the Church of the Open Door would come into view.

The church eventually sold its downtown property and moved to the suburbs. The building was eventually torn down. The sign ceased to burn. I never gave it much thought until one day when I was on my way from Pasadena to a meeting downtown and caught a glimpse of it in the corner of a salvage yard next to a stretch of the Pasadena freeway. There it was in a junkyard for signs. Hanging out among a community of cast-off logos for fast-food chains and gas stations was the now darkened proclamation "Jesus Saves."

The blazing message sent from the rooftop and the relative obscurity of its proclamation in the junkyard became for me not only a depiction of the essence of the gospel but also a reminder about where and how that word is preached. It was both a depiction of the truth of the incarnation and a reminder that there are no restrictions on the Spirit.

Holding together the image of the two locations of that sign and the nature of the "work" that it did in each place serves as an admonition to me. This metaphor is about seeing. It's about challenging the limits of my perceptions and my potentially stunted imagination. It's a call not unlike the one Jesus issues to John the Baptist in the wake of his question. "Go and tell John what you have seen and heard." In other words, "Go back and let John know that while I may not be doing what he thinks I should be doing, I am doing exactly what I said I would do." Here in Luke 7:22 Jesus revisits the announcement he made that day in the synagogue in Capernaum when he inaugurated his ministry by reading from the scroll of Isaiah:

> The Spirit of the Lord is upon me, because he has anointed me to bring good news to the poor. He has sent me to proclaim release to the captives and recovery of sight to the blind, to let the oppressed go free, to proclaim the year of the Lord's favor. (Lk 4:18-19)

The message Jesus gives to John's disciples is the reminder to be open to taking another look. Following John's expression of doubt, Jesus doesn't merely reassure him that he is okay and doing a good job. He challenges John, and it is in this challenge that we receive a second tool for dealing with the presence of doubt. What Jesus essentially does in this admonition is to invite John into a bigger world than the one he had previously perceived. He invites him to go deeper, to go beyond the limits of his expectations and perceptions and take another look.

This is the reminder we all need to hear. In the face of disappointment about who he is not, we need to be reminded to go back and take another look. We need to face into the truth of the limits of our perceptions and look again at who Jesus is revealing himself to be. Jesus' words are an invitation to contemplation, a call to awareness. His admonition is the gentle but powerful reminder that a great deal of the work we do as we follow him along the Way is to keep opening our eyes and ears to the truth of who he is. He can never be exhaustively described by us. There is always more about him to discover. The ingredients of mystery and humility are part of what fuels our journey with him.

The Cross as Our Focus

Paul issues a similar admonition to the Corinthian church in chapter one of his first letter to them. There he discusses the cross and refers to its apparent foolishness. He acknowledges that on the surface there doesn't seem to be much wisdom in it. However, he also invites the Corinthians to take another look at it. He asserts that this object of apparent foolishness is actually the embodiment of the wisdom of God. He reminds them that the cross has always been at the core of everything he has had to say: "When I came to you, brothers and sisters, I did not come proclaiming the mystery of God to you in lofty words or wisdom. For I decided to know nothing among you except Jesus Christ, and him crucified" (1 Cor 2:1-2).

In other words, "The most important word I have to preach is not an explanation of truth, it is an act of love. The thing to which I am compelled to direct your attention is a person and an event. The man hanging on the cross defies explanation, yet if you stand before this scene and try to take it in, you will see far more than any words of mine can ever depict."

There are aspects of this life in Christ that may initially make very little sense. Sometimes what we see yields more questions than answers. Yet Jesus responds to those questions not so much with explanations and answers as with the invitation to take another look at him. He never stops issuing this invitation, because all our explanations about him pale in significance next to the light he himself gives off.

The Pastor's Role in Invitation— and in Receiving Invitation

As prophets, we need to lead the way in reflecting this truth. In the face of our own dislocations and disappointments, we need to model this practice. In the face of the doubt and disillusionment of the people we serve, we need to demonstrate that our work is not merely to dispense explanations about God; it is more specifically to issue the unending invitation to pay attention to God.

Giving witness has a great deal to do with inviting people to take another look. Each Sunday as we craft a sermon and set that word in the context of worship, we are simply inviting people to see Jesus. Every time we meet with someone who has a question for or about God, we are given the opportunity to invite them to step back and look again. This practice never becomes tired or outdated, because we will never be able to contain Jesus in our perceptions or explanations. There will always be something more of God to discover.

In one sense, I suppose it is odd to think of uncertainty and mystery as fuel for Christian life and ministry, but coming to a place of doubt is often a key ingredient in inspiring us to move forward to a new place in our relationship with God. When my wife, Mary Ann, came to me with her observation about the effect on our family of my way of handling my vocation, I was invited into this mysterious space. I had to begin to engage the question of how the truth of what she was telling me was going to coexist with the call that I believed God had issued.

In our case, part of what helped me navigate this space was an invitation from another congregation to come and serve in a position where preaching was not going to be the primary focus of my work. Coming to a larger congregation where the intensity of preparing a sermon was no longer going to be the defining reality of my weekly rhythm helped me take a step back without taking a step away. It gave me the space to hold both voices in tension and receive the refining that came with acknowledging the truth of both.

When we are challenged to let go of our limited expectations about God and make space for a revelation of his true character, we are being invited by God into a place of new life and growth. It is not an easy journey. In fact, it feels pretty threatening. For like Peter rocking in that boat battered by the waves, we live with the apprehension that the one walking toward us on the water just might be a ghost. We're not at all sure it is Jesus, even though he is telling us, "Take heart, it is I; do not be afraid" (Mt 14:27).

Yet these are times that call for risk. The risk in Peter's

case was whether or not he would answer the invitation of the One coming toward him. The risk was to step out of the perceived place of safety, in Peter's case the boat, and walk toward the One who invites us to "Come." For me, that perceived place of safety was the pulpit. Like Peter's boat, it was the sure thing in my work. It was the place with which I was most familiar and most at home in ministry. To step back from it for a time initially seemed crazy. But I was hearing an invitation to trust that there was something more to God's call than the work I did from behind that pulpit.

I needed to learn that there was something about staying in that perceived place of safety that in the long run was actually going to keep me from truly answering God's call. In the wake of that decision to answer Jesus' invitation to step out of my own version of the boat, I can report that, like Peter, I was initially not at all clear about the One toward whom I was walking. I felt lost and angry about the decision I had made. There were times when I felt like I was sinking. Yet, as of this writing, I can report that the hand and the face of the One who issued the invitation did come into view. And it feels very good to be buoyed up by this One who is not merely who I imagined, but who has unequivocally shown himself to be the One I need.

9

CONFIDENCE

Receiving God's Blessing
Versus Seeking Approval

To what then will I compare the people of this generation,
and what are they like? They are like children sitting
in the marketplace and calling to one another,

"We played the flute for you, and you did not dance;
we wailed, and you did not weep."

For John the Baptist has come eating no bread and drinking no wine,
and you say, "He has a demon"; the Son of Man has come eating and drinking,
and you say, "Look, a glutton and a drunkard, a friend of tax collectors and
sinners!" Nevertheless, wisdom is vindicated by all her children.

LUKE 7:31-35

I was installed as the pastor of the congregation in Pasadena almost three years after my predecessor's departure. He had been pastor for almost twenty years, and the process of discerning that it was time for him to move on had been a bit of a mess. The fallout that greeted me when I arrived comprised hurt feelings, anger, fatigue, broken relationships and mistrust.

Of course, it will come as little shock to anyone that some people were happy to see him go; some realized it was his time to leave but were mad at the way he had been handled in the whole matter; and some saw no reason to have made a change in leadership. For the first group, he was a villain who had led the church into a steady state of decline. For the second group, he was a longtime friend who needed to be cared for. For the third group, he was just a part of what had always been, so why force a change, especially when he was so close to retirement. Irrespective of which group was right about him, he became in some sense the same thing for all three groups.

Through the conflicted process of saying goodbye to this longtime pastor, he became for that congregation something that he never should have become: the primary focus of the life of the community. The questions about his competence, style of leadership, needs, habits, practices and personality became the primary preoccupation of that community, and the work of attending to the presence and work of God in their midst fell into the background.

The Curse of the Approval Rating

This is not an unusual story. Much of this book has been about identifying some of the dangerous pathways that can deliver a pastor and a congregation into just this place. Both pastors and congregants play a role in ushering a community into this misdirected focus. What often produces this dynamic is that at some point pastors decide the most valid metric for gauging their success is their approval rating with the congregation, and congregants decide to gauge a pastor's worth in terms of whether or not their felt needs are being met by the pastor's ministry.

I suppose to some extent this measure has some validity in gauging the effectiveness of our work. After all, if the people to whom we are called to minister perceive that they are well cared for by their pastor, we must be doing something right. Yet if this metric is the sole arbiter of the effectiveness of our work, we are going to get into trouble, because ultimately it cannot sustain our journey with a congregation. It cannot give us the confidence we need to persevere, and it mutes the effectiveness of our prophetic work in that we march to the beat of the wrong drummer.

Any quick study of the lives of the Old Testament prophets reveals that they were not called to deliver the message that the people perceived they needed to hear; they were called to proclaim the message that God needed his people to hear. The moment we lose sight of this, we also lose connection with the energy that sustains our ministry. Confidence in God's call becomes replaced by confidence in ourselves and our ability to win the love of our congregation. When we make this shift, we become like addicts. Yet the controlled substance we pursue is the approval of our congregation, and as with addicts, the focus of our waking hours becomes the acquisition of enough of this substance to temporarily satiate our desire.

The taste of approval is sweet, but when it goes away fear can drive us to do all sorts of things in the often futile pursuit of the dream of getting it back. In short, we go after what we think will give us the confidence we need to sustain us in our ministry, and we end up on a quest that ultimately robs us of the very thing we need to persevere.

I must confess that in twenty-nine years of pastoral ministry I have not been able to overcome my taste for the approval of my congregation. Given the chance, I will be tempted to go after it every time. I remember with embarrassment my post-sermon ritual in the first congregation where I served as pastor. I would walk among the members during the coffee hour and visit primarily with those people from whom I knew I would get an affirming word about my sermon. Like a bee visiting the gardens that hosted the most pollen and nectar-rich flowers, I had my post-sermon path virtually imprinted in my autonomic nervous system. Buzzing about the church patio with a cup of coffee in hand and a smile on my face, I would land briefly among the groups of people who would contribute the highest yield of affirmation. I filled up on what I thought would sustain me before heading back into the sanctuary for the second service.

Thinking that comments like "You hit a home run on that one," "You're so insightful" or "I love it when you preach" would fuel my work, I placed myself to receive little shots of approval. And over the years in ministry, the pathways or opportunities to obtain this approval have only increased. I've gotten better and better at ferreting out untapped sources of this substance, and I know now that almost any pastoral encounter is ripe with opportunity to feed the insatiable demands of ego.

While it feels a bit strange to make such a public confession, I am freed to make it in that I know I am not alone. The narcissism that informs this quest for approval is something that I know I share with many, if not most, of my colleagues in ministry. Yet once this addiction is acknowledged and confessed, we face a dilemma as to what to do with it. A good starting place perhaps is to stand with the publican in Jesus' parable in his simple prayer, "God, be merciful to me, a sinner" (Lk 18:13). In humility, by the mercy of God, we can admit we are powerless over this addiction. We can admit to God and to ourselves that we are often motivated in ministry by self-interest.

Yet what we cannot do is remove ourselves from exposure to the sources that fuel our narcissism. A steady supply of both genuine gratitude and patronizing flattery is there for the taking in almost any congregation we serve. Thus the question before us is, What can help us ignore the bait? How do we accept the mercy of God, refuse the invitation to venture down this road of satiating our ego, and so avoid the path that ultimately leads both pastor and congregation to a place of destruction?

Deflating Our Egos by Remembering Our Call

I believe that the words of Jesus in Luke 7 give us a handle on navigating this dilemma. After replying to the disciples of John the Baptist and sending them on their way, Jesus turns to the gathered crowd with an admonition. His address to the crowd sends a message of affirmation about the ministry of John. What I hear embedded in this admonition is a message of encouragement to us as pastors. By confronting the crowd with the truth of their inconsistency and fickleness, Jesus helps us as pastor-prophets to put our quest for approval in proper perspective. Jesus' words here help us both uncover the lies we tell ourselves about those imagined sources of confidence and focus on the truths that help build real confidence in ministry.

Jesus begins this admonition with what essentially turns out to be a rhetorical question: "What did you go out into the wilderness to look at?" He offers his own set of answers to this question. In effect he says, "I know you didn't make the journey to see a reed swaying in the wind or someone dressed in nice clothes. You knew you weren't going to see a religious insider swaying in the winds of doctrine or an ecclesiastical functionary dressed up in the robes of political power. You knew you were going to see a prophet. You went because you wanted to hear the voice of God. You were hungry and hoping to consume the word that would satisfy you. You were tired and hoping to hear the word that would bring you life. You went out into the desert hoping to catch a glimpse of the real deal. And in John, that's who you saw: a prophet. In fact, you saw more than just any garden-variety prophet; you saw the one who gave witness to me."

As a pastor, what I hear in Jesus' words in Luke 7:24-28 is an encouragement to remember why we are in the business of giving witness to God. We do this because people need it. What's more, they expect us to do this. In short, people come to church because they are looking for God. According to Jesus, people made the journey out to the region surrounding the Jordan because they were in search of a prophet who could give them the word that would make sense of their lives. I believe we pastors need to rest in the truth that they show up in church on Sunday for the same reason.

For some reason, it is easy to lose sight of this. It's all too easy to put on the lenses of modern marketing strategies and begin to think that people have come to church primarily because they want a church, or a program, or a particular kind of worship experience. At one level, they probably do. Yet at a deeper, and sometimes unfelt level, they are compelled to come to church for reasons far more significant than this. We must keep in mind that the earthen vessel through which we serve the treasure of the good news is just that: a container, a delivery system. This vessel is not the point; it is the means of making the point.

I am not sure why we have fallen into the trap of believing that people are primarily in the market for a church. Perhaps we are still living out of the societal dynamics and assumptions of the post–World War II boom in church attendance in this country. In the face of decline, maybe we are looking for a way to preserve the particular shape of the institution that grew so strong in those years. This is obviously a question that is too big to be dealt with here. For now the observation to be made is that whenever we make the survival of the institution of the church the primary objective of pastoral ministry, we are starting down a road that leads to the very opposite result. When we decide to make the question of the attractiveness or marketability of the church the primary task of ministry, we begin to construct a contemporary version of what Jesus called "whitewashed tombs" (Mt 23:27).

I smile when I remember a worship survey we conducted at our church a few years ago. In the midst of a leadership transition, we decided we wanted to gain some perspective on the question of what our congregation was thinking about the style and effectiveness of our five worship services. We did so in the hope of gaining information that would help us reshape our worship services to better reflect the felt needs of our congregation. I worked with a team of elders and a professional polling firm, who designed a survey that we hoped would tell us what we were doing right and what might be missing in our current offering of worship services.

When the data came in and the report was written, I was

amazed by how little we discovered. The joke among those of us that worked on the project is that at the end of the day we uncovered the profound truth that the people of University Presbyterian Church like worshiping at the service they like to attend. This information and about $2.75 will buy you a tall triple Americano at Starbucks.

I am sure we made mistakes on this survey. No doubt, we could have done it better and it could have yielded more information than it did. However, I cannot escape the lesson that we were also barking up the wrong tree and expecting to find something that we could not discover in this way. Though we can take some pride in the attempt to be more aware and to be a more hospitable place for a greater number of people, the survey was not going to help us assess whether or not we were faithfully fulfilling God's call to give witness to the kingdom.

According to the survey, our approval rating among the congregation with respect to worship was pretty good, but this information did virtually nothing to give us the information that really mattered. Finding out what people liked or disliked about worship was not going to help us get at whether or not they were connecting with the truth that would set them free.

John's Call: Telling the Truth About Jesus

As I mentioned earlier, John the Baptist had pretty high approval numbers in his day. The market share of his ministry was huge. Yet he didn't set out to build a movement or create a new institution. He wasn't calling people to shun the traditions of worship in the temple and to follow him in the creation of some new sect of the faith. He was inviting them to a place of integrity and asking that they open their eyes to the incongruity between their religious practices and the actual state of their hearts. He was telling the truth that they all knew but needed to be reminded of. John was simply responding to the call of God to give witness to the coming kingdom, and people went out into the wilderness to receive the discomforting comfort of this messenger because deep within they knew this was exactly what they needed to hear.

It's amazing to think about the level of confidence we could have in ministry if we allowed our work to be fueled by the belief that people are actually searching for the Bread of Life and Living Water. Jesus' words to the crowd around him that day remind me that we have a product that people want, and they'll be drawn to it even if the packaging or brand doesn't initially catch their eye.

His words give me the confidence to be bold in ministry and "not lose heart" (2 Cor 4:16), because I can do my work in the knowledge that the treasure contained in the earthen vessel of the church is actually more attractive to folks than the container itself. While this is not to say I can completely ignore the delivery systems of ministry, it is to say that when I live in the confidence that people both need and want what I am pointing to, I can live with a little less anxiety about the means I am using to give witness to it.

Trusting the Message in a Fickle Market

So in this text Jesus indirectly tells us to trust our message and in so doing invites us to rest in the confidence that he is Lord. Yet as he continued in his admonition to the crowd around him that day, he in effect issued us another reminder that is equally valuable in building confidence for ministry. By admonishing the crowd for their inconstancy and fickleness, he also invites us as pastors to examine the metrics by which we evaluate our ministry. Jesus' words in Luke 7:31 and following seem to begin with a sigh: "To what then will I compare the people of this generation?" To paraphrase Jesus: "The presentation is never quite to your liking, is it? The package is never quite right. What speaks to you one day is the next day something that you find odious or off-putting. You are never fully satisfied, because in your judgment, there is always something else that could have and should have been done."

I am freed by Jesus' reminder that we serve in the context of a fickle and often unpredictable market. If our goal is to find the pleasure center of this market and keep feeding it, we will find ourselves chasing a moving target. The work of staying in touch with and implementing what is deemed to be culturally "relevant" is itself a full-time and often thankless, unproductive job. At the end of our careful research, meticulous design and flawless implementation of a new program, we can end up with something that fails to turn heads. For we arrive at our destination and find that the people we hope to attract to join us were there ahead of us and have already moved on.

While I was serving as pastor of worship in my church, I was deeply involved in the process of developing and hiring staff for a new style of worship service we began a few years before. At a point of absolute frustration and exasperation while I was conducting interviews for the worship leader of the new service, I put out a status update on my Facebook page that asked, "What does the word contemporary mean?

While you're at it, help me with authentic, modern and postmodern." I got all sorts of comments back from people, but my favorite came from a young-adult musician in our congregation who replied, "I've seen it most often mean 'failed attempt.'" How hard we try to discover and satisfy that thing that people are sure to like, only to offer it and find that it doesn't quite hit the mark.

In telling this story, I do not mean to suggest that the work of assessing the culture and seeking to communicate in relevant ways is without merit. Indeed, part of good ministry is living within a particular culture and understanding how to translate the gospel into its vernacular. John the Baptist himself is an example of doing just this. Staging his ministry out in the region of the Jordan was an absolute coup. It tapped into a well-known cultural story and invited people to reconsider their lives in light of it.

My point has more to do with the degree to which we give attention to this matter. If we spend too much time in anxiety over how we are going to say something or too much energy in the design of the package in which we are going to deliver something, we often end up obscuring the essence of the very thing we are trying to deliver. If the pleasure of our congregation is our primary concern, we quickly find ourselves in a place where we are spending so much time pursuing the winds of change that we fail to deliver what we have been called to dispense.

So I take heart in what Jesus says here, for he helps me release my death grip on a feverish attempt at control. In being reminded that I serve in the context of a fickle market, I hear an invitation to take my eyes off myself and look to him. For I can be assured, whether I give myself to the pursuit of the elusive goal of relevance in ministry or not, that I will wake up some morning to discover that my approval numbers have fallen because I failed to give the people of my congregation what they perceive they need. Living in anticipation of this is in its own way a call to relax and trust God. I need to set my sights on something bigger than the moving target of congregational approval. For the thing that sustains our work as pastors, the thing that gives us the confidence to persevere in the prophetic task and "not lose heart," has to do with the kingdom of God and not merely the judgments of human beings.

The Vindication of Our Work

Jesus' final phrase in this text is the icing on the cake: "Nevertheless, wisdom is vindicated by all her children" (Lk 7:35). In other words, "Remember, time will tell, and the truth will come out." In other words, relax in the truth that all things will be revealed. It's not in your hands, and the validity of your work will show itself, or fail to show itself, in time. So be faithful in the call to give witness to the kingdom and wait and see what God will do with the offering you have made.

The apostle Paul said something similar to this as he responded to the Corinthians' dissatisfaction with his ministry among them. As I noted earlier, much of Paul's second letter reflects his struggle to help the Corinthians understand the essence of his ministry among them. At points he has to defend himself against the charge that he is arrogant. As he deals with this charge in the third chapter he writes,

Are we beginning to commend ourselves again? Surely we do not need, as some do, letters of recommendation to you or from you, do we? You yourselves are our letter, written on our hearts, to be known and read by all; and you show that you are a letter of Christ, prepared by us, written not with ink but with the Spirit of the living God, not on tablets of stone but on tablets of human hearts. Such is the confidence that we have through Christ toward God. Not that we are competent of ourselves to claim anything as coming from us; our competence is from God, who has made us competent to be ministers of a new covenant, not of letter but of spirit; for the letter kills, but the Spirit gives life. (2 Cor 3:1-6)

In other words, God's work will show itself, and when it does, our work will be vindicated. Here is the ultimate source of our confidence: God is at work and nothing is going to stand in the way of that work. Along with Paul, we need to say to the congregations we serve, "If our labor among you has been valuable, that will become obvious in time, for the fruit of the Spirit will show itself in your lives. If anything we are doing has value, it is only because the Spirit of God is at work in us and through us to you. If we are participating in God's work among you, that will show itself in time. So take your eyes off us, and wait and watch for what God is doing in your lives."

The Grace of God Conquers Self-Doubt

As pastors, we would do well to apply the same advice to ourselves, especially in those times when we have fallen into the pit of self-doubt. We are often our own worst enemies when it comes to seeding things into our lives that destroy our confidence. The narcissism that sends us looking for congregational affirmation also sows the seeds of self-doubt and insecurity. When these seeds begin to germinate, the sound of our own voice commands more of our attention than the voice of God.

In the face of criticism, fatigue and failure, it is easy to forget that our ministry fits into the greater reality of God's story. It is easy to forget that we do our work in response to God's call and in the name of Jesus. Instead of seeing ourselves as participants in the work of God by the mercy of God, we myopically fixate on all that we are not, all that we might have been and all that we should be. The abstractions of our fears displace the concrete reality of God's love and grace, and like Elijah after his bout with the prophets of Baal, we are left with nothing but fatigue and the sinking feeling that we are alone (1 Kings 19).

There are potential invitations to self-doubt lurking around just about every corner in ministry, and ironically, some of the more profound invitations worm their way into us in the wake of great ministry success. This was certainly the case with Elijah. After having overthrown the prophets of Baal, and on the run because of the contract Jezebel had taken out on him, Elijah was spent and ready to die. "It is enough," he said. "Now, O LORD, take away my life, for I am no better than my ancestors" (1 Kings 19:4). At this point he was finished. He saw no way to go on. The thought of continued conflict or of having to be strong sent him into a dark place of depression. What he knew in that moment was his inadequacy, and there wasn't much room for anything else.

Enter the grace of God. The graces of food and sleep were the first rays of God's light that shone into the dark pit in which Elijah found himself. An angel appeared to Elijah with the obvious but easily forgotten advice: "Get up and eat, Elijah, and then go back to bed." Such is the first line of defense against ministry-induced depression. It is an illustration of the third psalm. With the message "There is no help for you in God" crashing into his consciousness and drowning out the possibility of hearing any other voice, Elijah did what the psalmist did: "I lie down and sleep; I wake again, for the LORD sustains me" (Ps 3:2, 5). Then and only then was Elijah ready to both express the content of his fear to God and to listen for a word of assurance from God.

What we know from this conversation between Elijah and God is that Elijah was in a space where he was having trouble listening to something other than the sound of his own voice. "I have been very zealous for the LORD. . . ; the Israelites have forsaken your covenant . . . and killed your prophets. . . . I alone am left, and they are seeking my life, to take it away" (1 Kings 19:10). In short, I've been faithful, they've been unfaithful, and I have no energy to continue to fight this battle by myself. Then God responded: "Go out and stand on the mountain before the LORD, for the LORD is about to pass by" (1 Kings 19:11). Be quiet; stop, look and listen for the signs of the presence of God. Then came the show: the great wind, the earthquake and the fire. And then after these, nothing but silence. The tacit question God powerfully posed in the silence was, "What do you hear now, Elijah?"

Elijah's answer was expressed in his actions. He got up, wrapped himself in his mantle, went to the mouth of the cave and began to listen. For what he heard, what he experienced in that moment, was the overwhelming awareness of the presence of God. What he knew then was that there is something far more substantial to pay attention to than the sound of his own voice.

A few years ago, the Getty Center in West Los Angeles hosted an exhibit of icons from the Monastery of St. Catherine on Mount Sinai. The exhibit was a treasure chest of some of

the oldest surviving icons that hang in that ancient monastery. One icon in particular became God's word to me that day. It was an icon of Elijah and the raven, depicting the scene in 1 Kings 17 when, during the great drought, Elijah was cared for by ravens who brought him bread and meat twice a day at the direction of God.

The icon itself is large, standing about five feet tall, and the figure of Elijah is impressive. He looks like the guy who called down fire on the prophets of Baal. In this depiction, he would make a good recruitment poster for the work of being a prophet. Yet what we soon focus on is not the prophet, but where the prophet is placing his attention. His eyes focus on a figure in the upper corner of the icon, and so the viewer's eyes are drawn to the same spot. There we see a raven. A raven that is way out of scale. It looks more like a ratty little blackbird. It has a morsel of bread in its beak. Then, above the raven, we see another image, an even smaller hand, the tips of its thumb and ring finger touching and thus forming the sign of a liturgical blessing of peace.

When we are in the business of talking, it isn't always easy to listen. Yet those of us who are called to give witness cannot do so unless we also come to attention. Our work as prophets is meaningless apart from the presence of the One who more often than not speaks with the still, small voice and offers us the sometimes indiscernible, gentle hand of peace. Therefore, if we are going to be about the work of pastoral ministry, we are going to need to cultivate the discipline of learning how to listen to something other than the sound of our own voices. We are going to need to learn how to wait and listen for the voice of God. When we are lost in the cacophony of self-generated messages about our qualifications or adequacy, we are robbed of all confidence to persevere in the work.

What we need to be reminded of in these moments is that the questions of our power and our adequacy for the task were never at the foundation of God's call in our lives in the first place. What was at the core all along was an invitation from God to participate in what he is doing. It is the gracious offer to turn our eyes away from ourselves, to focus on God and then to join with the other seven thousand who have not bowed their knees to Baal.

POSTSCRIPT

It's Not About You . . . or Is It?

[John] was a burning and shining lamp, and you
were willing to rejoice for a while in his light.
But I have a testimony greater than John's.

JOHN 5:35-36

It's not about you." We've all heard this admonition. Its application to our lives is broad. For our purposes here, it serves as the wake-up call that brings us back to the source of our life and the true substance of our ministry. Along with Isaiah, when we truly experience the holiness of God, it doesn't take long to have a corresponding awareness of our limits.[1] In the presence of God, all that we have to offer in and of ourselves pales in significance.

Yet as wise as this simple phrase is, there is something terribly superficial and incomplete about it. On the one hand, it is one of those truisms that we must heartily endorse. In the

---

[1] Isaiah's awareness of his "unclean lips" comes in response to his experience of God's presence and holiness. See Isaiah 6:1-6.

presence of a holy God, who can argue with it? However, if we are honest with ourselves, we must admit that the phrase nags at us. It demands qualification. It cannot be uttered without some corresponding explanation of the context in which we use it. Our experience tells us that there are ways in which ministry is about the minister. But how much of it is about us?

We spend our lives in ministry hearing from members of our congregation about the ways it has been about us. We are thanked for our insights and chastised for our lapses. We are blessed for the ways we have extended ourselves in love, revered for our wisdom and appreciated for offering a word that has catalyzed transformation in someone's life. We are also, however, excoriated for not coming through, for driving people away from the church forever and for failing to love enough at the right time in the right way.

In the face of these comments, we can swell with pride or wilt with shame. And both reactions are more about us than about God. Yet humility allows us to acknowledge that neither the complimentary accolades nor the derisive criticisms are ever the final evaluation of our ministry. For irrespective of our brilliance or bumbling, God will still be at work either through us or in spite of us.

Carrying a Light That Is Not Ours

I look at John the Baptist and I see the archetype of one who lived this tension. He is in this way the patron saint of pastors. He blazed a trail for us. He showed us what it means to hold in tension the Word that is wholly other than us and the unique means by which each one of us delivers it. Clearly, we are not the authors of the message we bring, yet neither are we merely mindless channels who act as inert conduits of God's message. We cannot do what we do apart from the Word that proceeds from the mouth of God, yet there is in our God-given personalities a uniqueness that gifts us and qualifies us for ministry.

Living on the line between these two realities is not an easy road to navigate. Yet John did it. Not always smoothly. Certainly not without questions and doubt. However, he still pictures for us what it means to seize a moment in ministry confidently while maintaining a grasp on the reality that this moment never fully belongs to us and lasts only for a time.

Jesus' line to the Pharisees in John 5 captures this tension for me. Here he affirms that for a time John did the good work of reflecting God's light. Yet the light John bore was derivative of a greater light: "He himself was not the light, but he came to testify to the light" (Jn 1:8). John gets a "well done, good and faithful servant" from Jesus. However, what is equally clear is that John is not the main act. His ministry had a beginning, middle and end. It was glorious in its day and contributed to the announcement of the kingdom. But it was only for a time, and the end of that time in no way hampered the forward march of the gospel and the coming of the kingdom of God.

The work of the prophet is only for a season. Our ministry has a shelf life. We give witness in space and time to that which transcends space and time. It's easy to forget this and fall prey to the mistaken assumption that what we have begun must continue, or what we have not yet finished must be completed. The joy of having a role in reflecting the light can easily morph into the lie that we are the light, and our ministry becomes more about preserving our ministry than about giving witness to the living God. We exchange the grand work of proclaiming the kingdom of God for the miniscule job of building a kingdom of our own. Instead of playing a part in God's story, we try to write our own.

In the face of this temptation, perhaps we would be helped by chewing on Jeremiah's prophecy about the new covenant. Here, through the prophet, God declares that with the institution of this new covenant, "no longer shall they teach one another, or say to each other 'Know the LORD,' for they shall all know me, from the least of them to the greatest" (Jer 31:34). I take some comfort in knowing that my job as a preacher will not be necessary when the kingdom comes in its fullness. (See also Is 54:13; Rev 21:22-27.)

Jesus didn't take up where John left off. He was and is the fulfillment of all that John proclaimed. Once John heard the Father's voice proclaim Jesus to be the beloved Son, it was time for John to step out of the way. Nothing is forever in pastoral ministry. What is forever is the gospel. What endures is the Word we proclaim. The people among whom we serve may appreciate the ways we reflect the light for a time. But our light pales when they see the greater light to which we give witness.

The Disappearing Pastor

I have a pastor friend who worked as a mountaineering guide before he was ordained. One time I heard him talking about what he loved most about leading people up challenging northwestern peaks like Mount Rainier. He said, "The best part is when we summit. You know what happens then? I disappear." I didn't get what he was saying at first. Thoughts of Scotty beaming him off the mountain ran through my mind. So he explained: "When we get to the top of the mountain, people don't immediately come up to me and thank me for guiding them. In fact, they don't even see me. What they do is rejoice in the exhilaration of having arrived at the summit. What they see is the view. And I get the privilege of watching them revel in their sense of accomplishment."

My friend's experience as a guide has also given him a metaphor for pastoral ministry. Pastor-prophets point the way. We help people find and navigate the trail to the summit. We cannot ensure they will arrive; we cannot carry them along the way. We simply do the work of pointing to the One who is the Way. What's more, when they do arrive, when they experience the embrace of the living Lord, we get the joy of knowing that we have been a part of God's work. We are witnesses to their joy and in that moment understand that the ministry we have is nothing more and nothing less than the gift of God.

Stupid Little Churches

I mentioned earlier that my seven years as pastor of Michillinda Presbyterian in Pasadena were lived out in a place that was one mile from a retirement home for Presbyterian ministers. The mixed blessing of this assignment was that along with lots of stories and lots of advice, I was given the gift of being able to contemplate my end. Living in the presence of men who had run the race and listening to their reflections about their lives in ministry gave me the opportunity to think about what I wanted to be celebrating when I was their age.

There were some among these pastors who primarily celebrated the growth of their churches. Often they spoke of their lives in ministry in terms of buildings built and the number of people (or "giving units") who filled them. During that post–World War II Protestant boom, these men and their wives walked into places where people were ready to find some kind of normalcy in the wake of worldwide chaos. They established congregations in the suburbs that were built to house the families who were doing their part to add to the baby boom.

Yet many of these congregations had become like the one I was serving. They hit their peak in 1968. Once there, they began a long and steady descent. The congregation I served had over seven hundred members in 1968, but when I came to be pastor in 1987 they had only about seventy people who regularly came to worship. In light of this decline, it was hard for me to celebrate the accomplishments of the men who told me about their growing congregations. Their monologues about success felt like empty reminiscence. It was clear to me then that celebrating the institutional markers of success was not what I wanted to be doing at their age. It was clear that there had to be something more enduring.

Fortunately, their example was not the only one I had. There were others who spoke not about institutional markers but transformed lives. One of these was a man who had pastored small congregations in Northern California mining and timber towns. Some stories were about the funny things that would happen in these rather rough towns. But other stories were pictures of hearts transformed by the power of God. And after telling me such a story, he would chuckle and usually say something like, "Can you believe it? People doing things like that, and to think they came from that stupid little church."

Most would not classify the congregation in which I currently work as a "stupid little church," since it has almost four thousand members. But I have come to believe that in God's economy, every congregation is a stupid little church. Whatever its size, every congregation pales in significance in the light of the kingdom of God. Furthermore, the work of those of us who serve these congregations becomes equally insignificant in this kingdom light. Yet while our work fades from view, it is not unnecessary or futile. It is essential, for our job is to give voice to the truth that wakes people up. Our job is to point and say, "Take a look at that. God is working and you can be a part of it."

Our Role in the Ongoing Story

The church in America is in an interesting place of transition right now. But I must confess to you that I spend little time reading sociological and organizational assessments of what is going right and wrong in the church. They are helpful in understanding the context of our work, and perhaps they even help shape the vernacular in which we deliver the gospel. But these works about the church tell us very little about the essence of our work.

We are not here to save the church. Our work is catalytic. Like a catalyst, it has value in that it fosters a reaction. Yet people will not remember what we said so much as they will remember what God did when we said it. Our delivery of the message has a shelf life. But if we don't deliver it, who will? If we don't take up the call God places on our hearts to invite people to consider truth that is bigger than themselves, then we miss out. We miss out on the incredible blessing and affirmation of participating in what God is doing.

It may not be about us. But God, in his mercy, invites us in to be a part of what he is doing. And there is nothing more affirming than this. We get to be that burning and shining lamp for a time. We get to engage the people who sit in pews of stupid little churches. We get to invite them to be a part of an adventure that is more magnificent than anything they could possibly plan for themselves. And we get to watch the transforming power of God usher them into their unique role in a story that only God could write.

Subject Index

Scripture Index